# CHRIST IN HIS
# FULLNESS

# CHRIST IN HIS FULLNESS

## BY BRUCE SULLIVAN

*CHRESOURCES*

*CHResources*
*PO Box 9290*
*Zanesville, Ohio 43702*
*(714) 450-1175*

*CHResources is a registered trademark*
*of the Coming Home Network International, Inc.*

*Bruce Sullivan*
*Christ in His Fullness*

*ISBN: 0-9702621-7-5*

*Cover design by Devin Schadt and David Griffey*

*Cover Photo by Marcus Grodi*

# Christ in His Fullness

# Dedication

To Father Benjamin F. Luther whose selfless dedication to the proclamation of the Gospel in both word and deed has been such a blessing to so many. Like St. Raphael with young Tobias, you have been God's guiding angel in times of testing. Your continued friendship has been one of God's greatest gifts and a treasured part of experiencing Christ in His Fullness.

# Acknowledgements

Numerous people reviewed the manuscript for this book and offered words of encouragement and helpful suggestions. While every one of them is greatly appreciated, three of them stand out in a special way: Father Ray Ryland, Marcus Grodi, and John O. Shields. Their fraternal support and guidance helped me carry this project through to completion. For that I am eternally grateful.

# Author's Notes

1. Unless Otherwise noted, all Scripture citations are from the *Revised Standard Version Catholic Edition*.

2. Unless otherwise noted, all Patristic citations are from W.A. Jurgens, *The Faith of the Early Fathers* (Collegeville, MN: The Liturgical Press, 1970). In addition, they have all been keyed to Jurgens' work by the letter "J" followed by a number that corresponds to the numbering in *The Faith of the Early Fathers*. Jurgen's work was selected because of its ease of acquisition and price.

3. Fictional names are so indicated by an asterisk (*) as they are introduced.

# *Prologue*

Mountains have long been a source of inspiration for the contemplation of God and our upward journey toward him. The Psalmist said, "I lift up my eyes to the hills. From whence does my help come? My help comes from the LORD, who made heaven and earth" (Psalm 121:1). And so I, too, lifted up my eyes on the beautiful Sunday afternoon of July 16, 1995.

I was participating in a division sales meeting for the company that was, at the time, my employer. The meeting was held in the picturesque setting of the Keystone Resort in the Colorado Rocky Mountains. Sunday was, of course, a "free" day for us, and I intended to take full advantage of it. My plans consisted primarily of trekking into the mountains for prayer, meditation, and spiritual reading. For reading material, I brought along a book on Eucharistic meditations.

On my way to the mountain trails, I was met by one of my co-workers, Joe*. We barely had exchanged greetings when, spying the book in my hand, he asked, "So, Bruce, what are you reading?" Before I could answer, he took the book from my grasp and began reading the description on the back cover. Returning the book, he commented, rather smugly, "You must be Catholic." I responded by saying, "As a matter of fact, I am." Not content to leave it at that, I quickly added, "But, I have not always been so."

Joe took a step backwards and said, "Really?" It was apparent that to him the idea of someone converting to the Catholic Faith

*A fictional name.

was rather strange and novel. After a moment's reflection he asked, "So, tell me this: What did you find in Catholicism that you did not find in Protestantism?"

Joe's question was a genuine one, and to be sure, quite a good one. Unfortunately, before I could begin to respond, some additional co-workers appeared on the scene and whisked Joe off to a white water rafting adventure. After that, Joe and I never had the opportunity to discuss his question. However, it stuck with me. What exactly did I find in the Catholic Church that I did not find in Protestantism? The following pages are my feeble attempt at an answer.

# Part I

*My Journey of Faith*

Chapter 1

# *"Jesus Christ is Not the Lord of Your Life!"*

Autumn on the campus of Auburn University in Auburn, Alabama, is truly exhilarating. Football is in full swing, a new academic year has begun, and the cooler weather brings welcome relief from the sweltering Alabama summer heat. Yet the crisp, cool air of the Auburn autumn often invites "heat" of a different kind – the heat of fiery outdoor campus preachers.

It was the fall of 1984. I was making my way across campus, smartly attired in my Air Force ROTC uniform, when I stopped to listen to one of those preachers. I had listened to several in the past and often, as in this case, they were traveling preachers making a circuit of major college campuses. Some of them could get quite comical, but there was little that was comical about this one.

He was serious and sobering to a degree that could, in fact, be described as grim. Clad in blue jeans and a T-shirt, with a carpenter's belt filled with tracts, he looked as if he had been transported by a time machine out of the 1960s. His wife sat off to the side, minding their two young children, her hair pulled back and covered with a bandana. He propped up a life-sized cross as he preached to the students going to and from their classes. His subject matter? Sin, judgment, repentance, and the need to save oneself from "the system." When personally challenged, he tended to respond with words of biting sarcasm.

I was simply one student in a crowd of dozens. Yet, this preacher singled me out in a rather profound way. He turned, looking directly at me, and said without sarcasm, *"Jesus Christ is not the Lord of your life! You're wearing it."*

I wasn't the only bystander wearing an ROTC uniform, so I began to object. However, an especially devout friend – also in uniform – encouraged me to simply *listen*. So I did. And as I listened, the Lord opened my heart to the truth of this traveling preacher's words, for indeed Jesus Christ was not, at that time, the Lord of my life. My pursuit of a particular career had become an idol.

I could not tell you that preacher's name; in fact, I don't think I ever saw him again. But I am convinced that God used him to speak to me at a very important juncture in my life. That juncture was one of coming to grips with the reality that each of us, at some point, must decide whether we will seek God's will or pursue our own. Sadly, we usually are not even cognizant that we are making such a choice. Prior to that day, I simply had assumed that my personal preferences coincided with God's holy will. I thank Him for the grace to have been shown otherwise.

There was nothing particularly earth-shaking about my upbringing. I was raised in the South as a Southern Baptist. In my youth, attending services three times per week was simply par for the course. My three sisters and I participated in children's choirs, Vacation Bible School, and youth group activities. At the age of ten, I made my first public profession of faith before the congregation of West Side Baptist Church in Hollywood, Florida, and from that point forward did my best to live the Christian life as I understood it.

I am eternally grateful to my parents, my grandparents, and the Southern Baptist Convention for introducing me to Christ, for rooting me in the Scriptures, and for instilling within my soul the conviction that what this world needs most is Jesus. However, it was not until I went off to college that I began to investigate seriously what I believed and why I believed it.

As is the case with countless others, my college years awakened in me a desire to put my Christian faith into action. Through my involvement in the Baptist Student Union, I was exposed to a wide variety of ministry opportunities and opportunities for spiritual growth. The bulk of my college years were spent at Auburn University. It was there that my spiritual journey began in earnest, sparked by a first-quarter elective course entitled "The History of Religion in America."

I am not sure what prompted me to enroll in that particular course, since it had nothing to do with my declared major. But I am certainly glad that I did, for it became the occasion for the first truly serious inquiry into what made me, a Baptist, different from the members of other Christian denominations. As a result, I began visiting the campus ministries of other denominations and, on occasion, even attended their worship services, while still actively participating in the Baptist Student Union and the local Baptist church.

The mere act of visiting Methodist, Lutheran, Presbyterian, and Pentecostal churches was not, for me, all that strange. My family, though Baptist, never instilled in me a strong sectarianism. We believed that good Christian folk can be found in all denominations and that one's particular denominational affiliation was not as important as having a close relationship with Jesus Christ. So when the opportunity to explore and investigate arose, I took full advantage of it.

For three years, I interacted with members of various denominations in order to investigate their distinctive claims and listened to a wide variety of campus preachers. In the process, I was shocked to discover to what extent my own theology had so many loose ends. So, I began searching. Searching for that which could tie it all together. Little did I realize that the words spoken in a chance meeting with a simple Arkansas traveler on a Greyhound bus were about to prove prophetic.

Chapter 2

# *From the Mouths of Babes and Old Men*

The bus trip from Montgomery to Auburn is a relatively short and usually uneventful route across East Central Alabama. On this particular January day in 1985, however, I was to have a most peculiar exchange with a fellow traveler.

I was on my way back to Auburn University after having attended Missions '85, a Southern Baptist missions conference for students in Nashville, Tennessee. Naturally, I was riding the crest of a wave of renewed religious enthusiasm, eager to engage any and all in a discussion of the Gospel.

Sitting across the aisle from me was a lean, weathered, elderly man in his early 70s. He was cordial enough but a man of few words. I tried to strike up a conversation but got few responses of more than two or three words. After some effort, I learned that he was from Arkansas and a member of the Church of Christ, but that was all. Upon discovering his church affiliation, I decided to question him about his beliefs.

I had always heard that members of the Churches of Christ thought that they were the only ones going to heaven. To a large degree, this understanding (or misunderstanding, as the case may be) is a matter of semantics. Part of their reasoning stems from their conviction that in the Bible membership in the church and the roll of the saved are one and the same. To be saved is, therefore, to be a member of the church, and the church described in the Bible is, in fact, the *"church of Christ."* The utilization of the lower-case "c" on "church" as if to make it something other than a denominational name is, however, a bit misleading. I say that because, in practice, the movement's adherents utilize the designation "church of Christ" in a sectarian manner by making the Biblical references to the "church of Christ" synonymous with the Church of Christ denomination that was spawned by the American Restoration or the Stone-Campbell Movement.

This movement, launched in the early 19th century, was so named for its two most prominent historical figures, Barton W. Stone and Alexander Campbell. They were driven by the desire to transcend denominational divisions and unite all believers in Christ on universally accepted essentials of the faith. Unable to achieve consensus of "universally accepted essentials," the movement eventually split into three denominations: the Christian Church (Disciples of Christ), the independent Christian Churches, and the Church of Christ. The modern-day Disciples of Christ emphasize the movement's early theme of Christian unity, whereas the independent Christian Churches and Churches of Christ tend to emphasize the theme of "restoration." Together, these three denominations can claim approximately four million present day members.

Furthermore, it is not uncommon to hear Church of Christ members say, "We are Christians only, but not the only Christians." Yet, when one studies what many Church of Christ members believe to be the definition of what qualifies one as a *true* Christian, it becomes apparent that they are the only ones that fit their description and thus, in practice, are the only *true* Christians.

I decided, therefore, to find out if the reports were true, so in the course of our conversation I asked him point-blank, "Can you go to heaven without being a member of the Church of Christ?" True to his simple, straight-forward form, he replied, "The Bible doesn't say you can." "Hmmm," I thought, "so the reports *are* true."

Well, we continued our chat, or rather I continued to talk, until finally he declared, "You seem like a sincere young man. I think that some day you will be a Church of Christ Gospel preacher." At this, I nearly fell out into the aisle laughing. "Me, a Church of Christ preacher? Not on your life!" That, at least, is what I thought.

Chapter 3

# I Just Want to Be a Christian

If you surf the television channels on any given Sunday morning, it doesn't take long to encounter religious programming of one stripe or another. That's the way it is today, and that's the way it was in 1985. Because I had grown interested in the beliefs of others, it was not unusual for me to view such programming before leaving for church. So I was following something of a routine that Sunday morning in January 1985 when I watched the *Amazing Grace Bible Class* broadcast from the Madison Church of Christ in Madison, Tennessee.

It had been about two weeks since my encounter with the elderly Church of Christ member on the Greyhound bus. I had given little thought to our conversation, but as the *Amazing Grace Bible Class* was going off the air, the thought occurred to me that in my exploration of different denominations, I had not yet visited the Auburn Church of Christ. So, that very morning I decided to rectify the situation.

Now, though I had not previously visited this church, I was not unfamiliar with the Churches of Christ. My best friend in high school was a Church of Christ member, and I had accompanied him to Sunday morning services on several of occasions (something for which my own pastor had severely rebuked me). At the time, my visits had amounted to little more than mere convenience or common courtesy. Now, however, my interest had progressed far beyond idle curiosity; I wanted answers.

My experience that morning at the Auburn Church of Christ was nothing short of enthralling. No, it wasn't the singing or the preaching, although both were superlative. It wasn't even the warm welcome I received from the congregation, for this was a common experience at nearly every church I visited. Rather, the height of the experience was the discovery of a truly kindred spirit: Jim Brinkerhoff, the congregation's remarkable campus minister.

Jim was leading a study of the book of Acts for college students when I arrived at Bible class that morning. It did not take long for me to realize that he was different from most of the other preachers I had encountered over the preceding three years of searching. Jim was knowledgeable but not a "know-it-all," he was confident but not condescending. He was enthusiastic about his beliefs but at the same time gentle in his presentation of them. Before the morning was over, I knew that in Jim I had found a man with whom I could converse without fear of rebuke or ridicule.

Before leaving the Auburn Church of Christ, I paid a visit to its literature rack, a practice I continue when visiting any church. I selected several pieces of literature that looked interesting. I still remember well the impact made by two of these tracts. One was entitled, "Neither Protestant, Catholic, nor Jew," and the other one was entitled, "The Old Path." These two tracts introduced me to what the Churches of Christ call the "Restoration Plea."

In a nutshell, the "Restoration Plea" is a call issued by members of the Churches of Christ to abandon man-made creeds and traditions for the purpose of restoring Christianity to its pristine purity. This "restoration" process includes "calling Bible things by Bible names" and "speaking where the Bible speaks," while at the same time "being silent where the Bible is silent." Church of Christ members believe that if these things are done, all New Testament believers will simply be "Christians only," and thereby experience true Christian unity. To be sure, there are other denominations that espouse a similar approach to Christianity. In the Churches of Christ, however, "Restorationism" is almost an exact science.

The *modus operandi* of this "science" is "patternism," which more than anything else describes the typical Church of Christ approach to the Scriptures. Under patternism, the New Testament writings are viewed as a set of blueprints or pattern. Then, using the New Testament Scriptures, Church of Christ members attempt to identify the elements of the "New Testament Pattern" for the Church. Underlying this approach to Scripture is the assumption that such is what God, by design, intended and that the details of the "pattern" are clear and unmistakable (the pitfalls to this approach will be addressed in Part Two of this book).

In comparison to the denominational chaos surrounding me, I found the "Restoration Plea" captivating. It seemed to hold the promise of cutting through all the alleged layers of religious accretions to bring one back to the authentic Christianity that Christ had established and Paul had preached. It held forth the promise that one could simply be a Christian and a Christian *only* by being lifted up above the denominational noise and confusion. Still, this "Restoration Plea" was something of a "hard sell" to someone raised in an evangelical tradition. To embrace it would require significant alterations of many doctrinal positions, resulting in real tension with friends and family members.

For example, as an evangelical Protestant, I had a rather fuzzy definition of the Church. Basically, I had been taught that the Church was an invisible, mystical body comprising all true believers from all denominations. We had rejected any idea that the Church had a distinctive, visible form associated with an identifiable institution as narrow-minded, sectarian, and, even worse, *Catholic*. Yet the Churches of Christ showed me that the Church, as depicted in Scripture, was a visible, identifiable institution. In fact, it was distinct enough to have, figuratively speaking, a *mailbox.* In other words, the apostle Paul could write to the churches at Corinth, Ephesus, Galatia, and Rome with a specific, identifiable group of recipients in mind. The logical conclusion, then, was to ask, "Is that institution still on this earth today, and, if so, where is it?" Thus the "Restoration Plea" prompted me to go beyond simply accepting the status quo; I was to search for the Church that Jesus had established—if it could, in fact, be found.

Also, as a Southern Baptist I was taught—and believed— that salvation was by faith *alone;* that once one was truly saved, salvation could never be lost or forfeited. It was Jim who helped me see that, according to the Scriptures, justification is *not* by faith *alone.* To my surprise, he pointed out that the only time in the entire body of Sacred Scripture where the words "faith" and "alone" occur together is in James 2:24, where we are told, "You see that a man is justified by works and *not by faith alone*" (italics added). Of course, the works spoken of are works of faith, but this serves only to underscore that saving faith is more than mere intellectual assent or personal belief. Saving faith is faith that *works* (Galatians 5:6). Or, to put it another way, the faith that *saves* is the faith that *obeys* (see Romans 1:5 and 16:26). Moreover, saving faith is faith that, through cooperation with grace, perseveres until the end (Revelation 2:10).

Nowhere are these principles brought together more clearly than in the exhorting words we find in Hebrews 3:12 and their surrounding context:

> Take care, brethren, lest there be in any of you an evil, unbelieving heart, leading you to fall away from the living God.

What is most significant here is that the entire third chapter of Hebrews is written to Christians (identified as "holy brethren"). These Christians, though already "partakers of a heavenly calling," were warned against the distinct possibility of falling away due to the hardness of heart that comes from the deceitfulness of sin (verse 13). The warning is given concrete form by the parallel traced by the sacred writer to the children of Israel who escaped bondage in Egypt only to die in the wilderness without entering the Promised Land. Moreover, in identifying why the children of Israel failed to enter the Promised Land, the sacred writer draws a distinct parallel between "disobedience" and "unbelief" (3:18-19).

As I continued to examine the "Restoration Plea" of the Churches of Christ, I came to see baptism in a way that differed significantly from my former understanding. Both Baptists and Churches of Christ teach that the *only* biblically correct mode for baptism is immersion (see Appendix E for further discussion of the mode of baptism). We both believe that baptism is of great importance, but as a Southern Baptist, I did not consider it essential to one's salvation. I believed that baptism was an entirely symbolic ordinance to which all Christians should submit in order to provide a public, outward testimony to an already existing internal reality. In other words, water baptism was *only* an outward witness to the new birth in Christ and not the means by which the new birth is conveyed to us.

Yet, as Jim led me through the Scriptures, I discovered numerous places where the language of Scripture depicts baptism as being more than merely symbolic. Specifically, what is symbolized *by* baptism is described as occurring *at* baptism, not before. For example, it is through baptism that we are buried with Christ in order that we might be raised up with Him to "walk in newness of life" (Romans 6:3-4). This newness of life begins when our sins are forgiven and washed away *in* baptism (Acts 2:38 and 22:16). As a result, we not only are raised up to walk in newness of life with Christ but also are actually "clothed with Christ" (Galatians 3:26-27). For this reason, the apostle Peter wrote that baptism *saves* us in the same way that the flood saved Noah and his family—by lifting them up from a world polluted by sin and setting them back down on a newly cleansed earth (1 Peter 3:18-21).

At this point, it should be noted that Churches of Christ are often mistakenly accused of preaching "baptismal Salvation" (as if they believed that baptism, not Jesus, saves one from sins). This came out when I was confronted by my Baptist pastor during the time in which I was considering the subject of how baptism factors into salvation. He replied, rather smugly, "Personally, I have always considered the blood of Jesus to be sufficient to wash away my sins." His implication? That the belief that sins are washed away at the moment of baptism amounts to a denial that it is the blood of Christ that cleanses us. That, however, is patently false. All Christians acknowledge that it's the precious blood of Jesus that washes away our sins. The question is: How and when does this happen? In other words, does it happen when we "come forward" in response to an "altar call"? Does it happen when we recite "the sinner's prayer"? Or does it happen when, in the exercise of faith in response to God's grace, we are baptized into Christ and, thereby, "born of water and the Spirit" (cf. John 3:5)? Moreover, the connection between baptism and the forgiveness of sins is rooted inextricably in the teachings of Sacred Scripture (as the references cited above demonstrate).

Such doctrinal adjustments did not come easily or without a price. For one thing, I was living in an apartment at the Baptist Student Center and earning my room by doing janitorial work in the building. To join the Church of Christ would mean having to find and pay for another place to live. But my Baptist upbringing had instilled in me a deep respect for the authority of Scripture and a desire to follow Christ wherever He might lead. As I studied with Jim, the scriptural evidence in support of these critical areas held by the Church of Christ continued to accumulate, and eventually, my mind became overwhelmed. Therefore, moved by the weight of the evidence and the exhilarating prospect of being a "non-denominational" Christian, I was rebaptized at the Auburn Church of Christ in February 1985. What I didn't realize at the time, however, was that I was on my way to becoming a Church of Christ "Gospel preacher."

Bruce & Gloria on their wedding day at
the Auburn Church of Christ.

# Chapter 4

# *What God Has Joined Together*

Constructed of rough-hewn beams from the surrounding hardwood forest, the Old Mulkey Meeting House in Monroe County, Kentucky, is the oldest log meetinghouse in Kentucky. It was built in 1804 by the Mill Creek Baptist Church during a period of fervent revival. Many Revolutionary War soldiers and early pioneers, including Daniel Boone's sister, Hannah Pennington, are buried in the churchyard. Its historical significance, however, goes much deeper than its age and the notoriety of those interred in its graveyard.[1]

On Saturday morning, November 18, 1809, John Mulkey, preacher for the Mill Creek Baptist Church, stood before the congregation of two hundred and said, "Now all you who believe as I do, follow me out the West door."[2] With that, some one hundred and fifty members of the Mill Creek Baptist Church sided with John Mulkey in a religious controversy that was just building up steam. The preaching of Alexander Campbell, Barton W. Stone, John Mulkey, and several other like-minded individuals was about to launch what has become known as the Stone-Campbell Movement or the American Restoration Movement. From this movement, three different denominations were eventually formed: the Christian Church (Disciples of Christ), the independent Christian Churches, and the Churches of Christ.

The Stone-Campbell Movement swept through Kentucky like a prairie fire, making converts wherever it went. To this day, Kentucky is considered a stronghold for all three of its associated denominations. It has been said that there are more Church of Christ members per capita in Monroe County, Kentucky, than anywhere else in the world.

Less than twenty miles from the Old Mulkey Meeting House, in neighboring Metcalfe County, Summer Shade is home to a sturdy people that still possess the independent, pioneering spirit of their ancestors and a deep sense of history. The Stone-Campbell Churches of Christ have a rich heritage in this rural community, especially in the family of Gloria Ann Edwards.

Gloria's family has roots in the Stone-Campbell movement that are deep and strong. Her great-grandfather was an elder in a local Church of Christ congregation, and her grandfather donated the land on which that same congregation's church building was constructed. As a young girl she drank deeply from the well of religious instruction and became a dedicated and devout member of the Church of Christ.

In the autumn of 1982, Gloria began her studies at Auburn University's College of Veterinary Medicine. Despite the grueling demands of the curriculum, Gloria became an active member of the Auburn Church of Christ and its campus ministry, the Auburn Christian Student Center. Always faithful in her attendance, she was present at the Sunday evening service in February 1985 when I was baptized. At that point, we had not been introduced, but sixteen months later we would stand together in that same house of worship to be joined as husband and wife.

Chapter 5

# Into the Sunset

Some places in the world are known by their dominant topographical features. You cannot visit Paris and miss seeing the Eiffel Tower. You cannot cross over the Mississippi River into St. Louis and not take note of the 630 foot tall Gateway Arch. And you cannot visit the campus of Auburn University and not notice the dominant topographical feature of east central Alabama: Jordan-Hare Stadium, with its seating capacity of more than 85,000. Likewise, you cannot visit the Sunset Church of Christ in Lubbock, Texas, and not notice the Flag Room. Featuring flags from well over 100 nations, the Flag Room underscores the Sunset School of Preaching's dedication to world evangelization. When I was a student there from 1986 to 1988, there were flags on one wall representing the 96 different nations to which former graduates had gone in the school's 25 year history. On another wall were flags from nations targeted for future efforts.

The Sunset School of Preaching was established in 1962 under the oversight of the elders of the Sunset Church of Christ. First known as Latin American Bible School, the school had also been called West Texas Bible School before it received its current designation in 1995 of the Sunset International Bible Institute. More Church of Christ preachers have been trained at the Sunset School of Preaching than at any other school. Furthermore, among Churches of Christ, no other institution can claim greater success in training men and women for service as missionaries. Therefore, Jim, knowing of my desire to serve our Lord as a missionary, began steering me toward Sunset from the moment of my baptism.

The training program at Sunset was a demanding one. Students complete 120 semester hours of biblical studies in a two-year time frame. Due to time constraints alone, part-time employment was generally out of the question, and since most of the preachers-in-training were married men with families, financial assistance was a necessity. It was an accepted practice for prospective students to solicit support from local Church of Christ congregations. Consequently, Gloria and I spent our first summer as husband and wife raising financial support so we could enroll as students in the fall. By summer's end, we had loaded everything we owned into our 1980 Chevette and headed west in preparation for an anticipated lifetime of missionary service.

The Sunset School of Preaching more than met our expectations. The curriculum was intense, the camaraderie was palpable, and the experience was profoundly life-changing. For two years we were the privileged pupils of men who had given their lives to missionary service all around the globe. Their examples served only to heighten our own desire for missionary service. As a result, we became charter members of a missionary team bound for the largest Catholic nation in the world—Brazil.

We selected Brazil because, at the time, we believed that Catholics, more than anyone else, stood in need of the "true" Gospel of Jesus Christ instead of the allegedly "false" gospel of the Catholic Church. The majority of our instructors at Sunset had spent significant portions of their lives as missionaries in countries that were predominantly Catholic. While possessing a sincere and deep love for Catholic people, many of them expressed a palpable contempt for the Catholic Church and her teachings. This, coupled with the influences of anti-

Catholic groups I had encountered in college, gave me a less than complimentary view of the Catholic Church. In my mind, Catholics were superstitious, idolatrous children of the Whore of Babylon who could not be regarded as true Christians. I also believed that the ranks of the Catholic clergy were filled with corrupt, deceitful men who were damning the souls of untold millions because of their perverse teachings.

Upon graduation from Sunset in June 1988, Gloria and I moved to Kingsport, Tennessee, to work with the Colonial Heights Church of Christ. The good brethren at Colonial Heights had supported us in our studies and had agreed to be our sponsoring congregation when it came time for our mission team to go to Brazil. The plan was for each of the mission team families to work with a sponsoring congregation for two years before departing for a five-year commitment in Maceio, Brazil. Those two years would give us time to gain practical ministry experience, study Portuguese (the language of Brazil), and provide opportunities to develop a working relationship with our sponsoring congregation. It was a good, solid plan formulated by a group of veteran missionaries.

Less than a year after graduation, however, our mission team disbanded. This disruption in our missionary dreams led us to move to Greenville, North Carolina, to serve in the campus ministry of the Greenville Church of Christ, an outreach to the students of East Carolina University. We still planned to one day link up with another mission team, but we felt that serving in a campus ministry would bear much fruit for our Lord. What made this move different for us was that it was no longer just the two of us: our first child, Mary Elizabeth, had been born during our year of service in Kingsport.

In time, the financial needs of our young and growing family cut short our stay at Greenville. Interestingly enough, while members of Catholic religious orders take an *explicit* vow of poverty, most Protestant ministers *implicitly* do the same. But when we began to pay for necessities with credit cards, we knew it was time to change gears.

Determined to keep Gloria at home with our daughter Mary, I decided to seek employment outside the ministry. Since my degree from Auburn was in agriculture, I applied for and received a position with the University of Kentucky College of Agriculture's Cooperative Extension Service. I became the County Extension Agent for 4-H and Youth Development in Hart County, Kentucky, only thirty miles from Gloria's home in Metcalfe County.

Though not full-time, we continued to serve actively in our local congregation. I preached and taught Bible studies on a regular basis, as it is not uncommon for preachers in rural areas to support themselves by means of secular employment. And true to the vision instilled in us at Sunset, we continued to look for the opportunity to join a mission team bound for South America.

# Chapter 6

## *Apples, Apples Everywhere!*

The young farmer was no greenhorn. He had taken apples to market many times in the cart that had been passed down from his grandfather to his father, and from his father to him. The old applecart had always proven reliable in the past, so he had no reason to think that today would be any different. Today, however, *was* different. Maybe he had loaded it with just one too many apples. Maybe the wood of the cart handles had dry-rotted or had become worm-eaten. Maybe the young farmer simply lost his balance and stumbled. In any event, before he knew what was happening, the handles of the cart snapped, the cart tipped, and apples were rolling everywhere.

When I accepted the position as County Extension Agent, I had no intention of hanging up my spurs as a "Gospel preacher." After all, once a preacher, always a preacher.

There were numerous opportunities open to me as an itinerant preacher, from filling the pulpit at various congregations or teaching Bible classes, to helping with hospital and home visitation. We even went on short-term missionary trips, like the one to Haiti in 1993. The most surprising opportunity, however, was the Extension position I held for the county. This placed me in close contact with numerous families, providing chances for service that otherwise may never have materialized. One such family was that of Art and Sharon Antonio.

Art Antonio, a native of the Philippine Islands, was a twenty-one year veteran of the U.S. Navy. When he retired in 1990, he and Sharon fled from the urban jungle to raise their children in a more peaceful and wholesome setting. Their search led them to a farm in Hart County, where I met them in my official capacity as a county Extension agent. As I grew to know them and their family, I could not help but notice their deep and sincere Catholic faith. I felt a tremendous burden to reach out to them with the "true" Gospel. I remember thinking, "It would be a real shame to see such devout people go to hell." As a Church of Christ member, I believed that Catholics were unsaved because they had not obeyed the "pure" and "simple" Gospel of the New Testament, but had embraced a false religion with origins in the very pit of hell.

For the better part of a year, I did my best to engage Art and Sharon in discussions about Christianity and the Bible in order to show them the "true" Gospel of Christ as taught by the "true" Church of Christ. Our conversations, however, were continually plagued by interruptions, misunderstandings, and hurt feelings. Finally, in early June 1993, exasperated, I attempted to engage in a bit of "charitably motivated manipulation." I told Mrs. Antonio, "Look, if you—or anyone else—can show me *from the Bible* that the Catholic Church is the Church established by Christ, I'll become a Catholic tomorrow!" With that bold statement, I presumed to goad Sharon into a serious Bible study. Instead, she handed me a copy of Karl Keating's *Catholicism and Fundamentalism.*[3]

I was elated and took this as an indication of interest. We might just be getting down to brass tacks after all! In my mind, when she gave me that book to read, she also was giving me license to come back and "critique" it—that is, to expose the manifest errors that I knew, *a priori*, it must contain. When I got home, I perused the back cover and saw a statement by Sheldon Vanauken: "I strongly advise honest fundamentalists not to read this book. They might find their whole position collapsing in ruins." I broke into hysterics, laughing out loud. But I didn't laugh for long.

I was leaving for a three-day 4-H conference in Lexington that promised to afford ample time for reading, so I took the book along. At the end of the trip's first day, I telephoned home and told Gloria, "We're in trouble. This guy is asking questions that I can't answer." Gloria responded by saying, "Well, you just go ahead and study, because I have some questions that I can't answer either." By the time I returned home from the trip, I had devoured Keating's book. In the process, my cart had been unexpectedly overturned, and I found myself scrambling to gather up my apples.

Reading *Catholicism and Fundamentalism* unexpectedly overturned my overloaded, anti-Catholic applecart in at least three ways. First, the book devotes eight chapters to examining the writings and ministries of several prominent anti-Catholics. In so doing, Keating documents the numerous ways in which professional anti-Catholics have repeatedly maligned the Catholic Church, by presenting false caricatures of the Catholic faith and distorting the facts of history. For example, one anti-Catholic source claims that the Inquisition took the lives of *95 million* people.[4] Yet there were not even 95 million people living in all of Europe at the time of the Inquisition! Distortions like this are legion, and readers are referred to Keating's book for additional examples.

The exposure of the outlandish nature of such prejudicial concoctions had a profound effect on me. I was forced to admit that many of the men in whom I had placed confidence, well known preachers whom I considered heroes, were, in fact, unreliable. Furthermore, it underscored that many of my gut feelings about the Catholic Church had their origins not in fact but in fiction. As a result, I recognized the need to hear "the rest of the story."

Second, Keating's book did what I thought no one could do: present from the Bible a convincing defense of the Catholic faith. Having never heard a solid, biblical defense of the Catholic faith, I assumed that none existed. While it is true that I had studied Roman Catholicism at Sunset under the tutelage of men who had many years of experience in Catholic cultures, those studies were tainted by anti-Catholic prejudice—both on their parts and on mine. Did we learn the Catholic faith from Catholic sources? No. In being trained in the techniques of "demolishing" the Catholic faith, did we study any Catholic apologetics materials to hear the best arguments that could be put forth by Catholics? No. Is any of this at all surprising? Not really. This is fairly typical across denominational lines. Rarely do the leaders of the various denominations invite representatives from the "enemy camp" to make presentations to their people. Instead, they simply present their predigested version of what they want their flocks to hear, seeking ever and always to protect the sheep from what they might not be "mature" enough to handle. The result is that people often think they know what others believe and the extent of their arguments, when in reality their own perception is colored by the lens of ignorance.

By way of example, one of my instructors from Sunset, upon hearing that I was considering the Catholic faith, initiated an exchange of letters in the hope of dissuading me from becoming Catholic. The main Catholic teaching he chose to attack was the perpetual virginity of Mary. In one of his letters he surmised that the Catholic Church teaches that Mary was perpetually a virgin because, being immaculately conceived, her other children and their descendants would all be conceived immaculately as well, something that would prove a bit problematic to the Church. The obvious difference, however, between Jesus and any other children that the Blessed Virgin could have conceived would have been the existence of a fallen human father. This is fairly basic, but my former instructor, who was ostensibly an expert on Catholicism, could not grasp it. This is not unique. I have yet to hear any "expert" anti-Catholic correctly present the Catholic faith.

Finally, *Catholicism and Fundamentalism* exposed the flimsy nature of the presuppositions underlying my Protestant faith. These presuppositions pertained primarily to authority, the Bible, and the Church. In other words, his book was the first occasion for an intense and critical consideration on my part regarding the standard Protestant operating assumption of *sola Scriptura*, or the belief that the Bible only, without the Church, is the sole guide for Christians in all matters of faith, morals, and practice. While I had memorized Bible verses that appeared to establish the teaching, I found that the doctrine was largely *assumed* as being self-evident, as were my personal interpretations of the standard proof texts. Obviously such a foundational doctrine cannot simply be assumed.

Keating's book, therefore, raised the question, "Where does the Bible actually teach the doctrine of *sola Scriptura*?" Closely related to that question were two others: "How do I know that my understanding of the Scriptures is correct?" and "How can I have infallible certitude regarding the canon of Scripture apart from the teaching authority of the Catholic Church?" Try as I might, I could not get these three questions out of my mind, nor could I avoid their implications. More than anything else, they sent the apples rolling (these questions will be addressed in detail in Chapters 11 and 13).

When I returned Keating's book to Mrs. Antonio, she asked, "Did you read it?" Unprepared to admit the full extent of the book's impact, I simply said, "Yes." I did, however, mumble something to the effect of, "I have some things to think about."

Picking up on this, she responded, "You need to meet Father Benjamin Luther. He's a former Church of Christ member, and the Fathers of Mercy at South Union can help you get in touch with him."

The Congregation of the Fathers of Mercy at South Union, Kentucky.

## Chapter 7

# *The Lutheran Connection*

O verlooked on many maps and located in the heart of South Central Kentucky's gently rolling farm country is South Union, Kentucky. It is home to a grain depot, a farm supply store, a used farm implement dealer, and the Fathers of Mercy. From this seemingly sedate and obscure setting, the Fathers of Mercy set out on a daily basis to impact the world for Christ in a way that few others can claim.

Formed in 1808 in response to the crisis of faith precipitated by the French Revolution, the Fathers of Mercy originated in France then came to the shores of America in 1839. Now, in response to the crisis of faith brought about by rampant secularism, materialism, and modernism, the Fathers of Mercy tirelessly travel throughout our nation preaching parish missions that are catalysts for authentic renewal in the Church.[5] When they moved their base of operations to South Union in 1988, they found a true friend and *compadre* in Father Benjamin F. Luther of the Diocese of Owensboro. At Mrs. Antonio's suggestion, I telephoned the Fathers of Mercy in June 1993, looking for information on how to contact this Catholic priest called, by of all names, Luther.

A native of Mayfield, Kentucky, Benjamin F. Luther was born in 1931, the son of Leon and Mattie Luther. Though born into a family with a rich heritage in the Stone-Campbell Churches of Christ, Ben Luther began his journey to the Catholic faith as a teenager. At the age of seventeen he was received into the Catholic Church, and after serving a tour of duty with the U.S. Navy, he completed his seminary training and, in 1964 at the age of thirty-two, was ordained a priest for the Diocese of Owensboro.

Because of his upbringing in the Church of Christ, Father Luther has always had great respect for his separated brethren in the Stone-Campbell Movement and a great interest in their history. In fact, he is most likely the only Catholic priest who is a lifetime member of the Disciples of Christ Historical Society.[6] So when I contacted him in June 1993, he was more than enthusiastic about helping me. At the time, he was pastor of St. John the Evangelist parish in Paducah, Kentucky, more than 200 miles from where Gloria and I lived. Nonetheless, within a week of our first telephone conversation, we were seated together at a roadside diner off Interstate 65 in Hart County.

Our first meeting lasted just a bit over six hours (I've always wondered what the waitress thought about those two guys talking non-stop theology for six hours at her work station.) At first, like any average Church of Christ fundamentalist, I was more than reluctant to address him as "father." I had been taught that the Catholic practice of calling priests "father" was a blatant violation of biblical teaching. For quite some time, I had considered it an obvious "red flag" that clearly demonstrated the apostate nature of the Catholic Church. To quell my queasiness, Father Luther helped me see that the passage normally cited by Protestants to denounce this practice, Matthew 23:1-12, cannot be used to attack the Catholic faith without indicting the Apostles and the early Church as well (see Appendix F for more discussion of this issue).

In the course of that first meeting, we broke plenty of ground for future discussions on authority, the Scriptures, the nature of the Church, Church history, and the writings of the Church Fathers. Before we parted company at the end of the day, Father Luther gave me a box containing various books and articles for study, which were but a foretaste of things to come. From that day onward, my mailbox was rarely empty. Father Luther would send me a book one day, a personal letter a couple of days later, and maybe a set of audiotapes a day or two after that. He sent Gloria and me a complete set of back issues to *This Rock* magazine[7] that served as a virtual course Catholic apologetics. Moreover, on Saturdays we would have telephone conversations that often lasted two hours or more and always on his "nickel."

Nevertheless, my struggles did not just magically disappear with the arrival of Father Luther. They had only just begun. The questions raised by Keating's book would lead to still further questions, and the standard list of controversial Catholic teachings on the papacy, the Eucharist, purgatory, Mary, the communion of saints, and Sacred Tradition still needed to be addressed. Historical concerns, such as the Inquisition and the Crusades, would require careful attention. Preconceived misconceptions would need to be identified and dispelled. Moreover, numerous encounters with presumably well-meaning Catholics would come awfully close to scandalizing me (since the subject of scandalous conduct by professing Catholics can be understandably troubling to many inquirers, I've addressed this subject in more detail in Appendix D). All of this would require time and study, but more than anything else, it would require what God is always ready to give: *grace*.

Chapter 8

# *Peter, Paul, & Mary*

The *Coming Home Network International*[8] began in 1993 out of the seemingly isolated experiences of several Protestant clergy and their spouses. Upon leaving their pastorates to enter the Catholic Church, these clergy and their families discovered with surprise that there were many others being drawn by the Holy Spirit to make the same journey "home." To help bring these inquirers and converts together, a simple newsletter was started, and gatherings and retreats were scheduled. The first retreat was scheduled for December 10-12, 1993, on the campus of the Franciscan University of Steubenville in Ohio. Father Luther suggested that it might be beneficial for me to attend the retreat with him. He was right.

Being the first retreat of an organization that was only six months old, the 1993 Fall *CHNetwork* retreat did not have many participants. In addition to Father Luther and me, there were about six or seven married couples, all of whom were Protestant clergy converts to the Catholic faith. They included the founder of the *CHNetwork*, Marcus Grodi, and his wife, Marilyn; Fr. Ray Ryland (a converted Episcopal priest and the chaplain for the *CHNetwork*) and his wife, Ruth; and Scott Hahn (Professor of Theology at Franciscan University) and his wife, Kimberly. These couples have all since become cherished friends.

I must say that I was especially pleased to make the acquaintance of Scott Hahn because three months prior to the retreat, Fr. Luther had given me Scott's audiotape series, "Answering Common Objections to the Catholic Faith."[9] This series was instrumental in helping me see the Catholic faith in a beautiful, new light. Before I listened to this series, the issues were all somewhat academic and, for the most part, I was searching for the Achilles heel of the Catholic faith (in order that I might remain comfortably where I was in the Church of Christ). That posture changed, though, when I listened to Dr. Hahn's tape series. His presentations brought out not only the evidence for the Catholic faith but underscored the *beauty* of the Catholic faith as well.

When I arrived at the retreat, I quickly discovered that I was the only participant who was not yet Catholic. I had been studying for several months, and my studies had already led me to conclude that a principal Protestant operating assumption, *sola Scriptura,* was untenable, unworkable, and, ironically, *unbiblical* (see Chapter 11 for more details on the problems of *sola Scripture*). Many of the presuppositions underlying my Church of Christ beliefs had been shown to be lacking. I had also come to the point of recognizing the beauty of many Catholic teachings if they could be shown to be *true*. As it was, I no longer believed that I had to be a member of the Church of Christ in order to get to Heaven, but that did not mean that I was certain that I could get there as a Catholic. In other words, the rejection of my former position did not necessarily mean I was prepared to accept the Catholic faith. Therefore, though I arrived at the retreat with an open heart and mind, I was still "kicking against the goads." That, however, was about to change.

For months I had been studying, praying, and contemplating, consumed by a desperate need to know the truth. Karl Keating's book had overturned my applecart, and the shortcomings of the

"Restoration Plea" had been laid bare. Yet I was at an impasse. It was as if I could argue both sides of the issues, a conundrum that is particularly frustrating for a preacher accustomed to "black and white" clarity. One of my biggest fears was that of being left in a state of perpetual gray without any clear-cut answers.

Often, I would go for long walks in the woods behind our house to pray and mull over the results of my studies. I can remember telling our Lord, "I will believe whatever You want me to believe…just please make it clear." Moreover, I was horrified by the thought of leading my family into making a potentially soul-damning error. But the questions would not go away, and only the Catholic Church seemed to offer any hope of providing satisfying answers. At times, this internal tension seemed almost unbearable. By the time I arrived at the retreat, I was near the point of cognitive overload.

In the setting of that retreat, it became clear that while the apprehension of truth involves the use of reason, reason unaided by grace can take one only so far. Mind you, this was not a completely new revelation to me; after all, as a Church of Christ preacher I had been taught to study God's Word prayerfully, asking God for wisdom and understanding. My studies, however, had driven me nearly to the point of paralysis, and the classic "Ben Franklin" method of decision-making simply was not working. At some point in my early years, I was taught that Benjamin Franklin made decisions by dividing a piece of paper into two columns: one for "pros" and the other "cons." He then would make his decision based upon whether the "pros" outnumbered the "cons." I don't know whether Mr. Franklin actually did this or not, but the method was one I had used often, yet now it wasn't working. I needed help—supernatural help.

On the second day of the retreat, I awakened rather early in the home of my host family and went downstairs while everyone else was either asleep or occupied with the start of a new day. Passing quietly down the hall, I noticed a small prayer closet off to the side of the living room. It was a rather small niche with a kneeler, various holy images, and candles. In the dark, quiet solitude of that moment, I was drawn to prayer. This time, however, my prayer would be a little different from any prayer I had ever offered.

I remember thinking to myself, "If what the Catholic Church teaches about the communion of saints is true, then maybe this is the time to enlist the prayers of the saints in heaven." In my readings, I had discovered that belief in the communion of saints was attested to in the first-century Apostles Creed and simply refers to the Catholic teaching that all the members of God's family (the saints on earth, the souls in Purgatory, and the saints in Heaven) comprise one Mystical Body of Christ. As such, they are mindful of one another and enjoy communion with each other in Christ. Therefore, the saints on earth pray for the souls in Purgatory while, at the same time, enlisting the prayers of the saints in heaven on their own behalf.

This, of course, was a new idea to me, but it was not necessarily a strange one. After all, at every church in which I had been a member, prayer requests were presented and members brought their needs before their fellow believers, asking for intercession. In so doing, they were not denying their freedom in Christ to directly approach the throne of grace (Hebrews 4:16). Rather, they were acknowledging what St. Paul himself recognized— that it is God's will that we intercede for one another and that He responds to such intercession. Often, St. Paul earnestly sought the prayers of the saints on earth, as is seen in Ephesians 6:19, Colossians 4:3, and I Thessalonians 5:25. Could he, and did he, pray directly to God? Of course he did, but this did not stop him from enlisting the prayers of others, which would have been a waste of time if, in fact, there was no benefit to it.

Furthermore, since the Scriptures teach that it is the prayer of a "righteous man" that "availeth much" (James 5:16), such intercessory prayer is not usually solicited from those who are regarded as disreputable and immoral. Combine these principles with the fact that the saints in heaven have been forever perfected in Christ and that, having been perfected, they are continually before the throne of God in worship and prayer (Revelation 7:12–8:4), and you have the reality of the communion of saints.

Kneeling in that little niche, I approached the Father's throne of grace—in the name of Jesus—asking for the grace of clarity and understanding. I had done this more times than I could count over the preceding six months of struggle, but for the first time, I concluded by asking the saints in heaven to pray for me as well. Specifically, I solicited the prayers of Peter, Paul, and yes, Mary. To cover all bases, I also was quick to ask God to forgive me if such an action offended Him. I did this because, while my studies had sufficiently demonstrated the intellectual veracity of the Catholic teaching, the outward, concrete expression of the teaching ran against the emotional grain of my Protestant upbringing. What was about to follow during the next hour, however, would assure me that Sts. Peter, Paul, and Mary had indeed heard my plea, and in response to their prayers, God was pouring out His grace.

Back on the campus of Franciscan University, our retreat resumed in the campus chapel with all of us participating in the early morning Mass. I had attended Mass a couple of times before, but could never get past my knee-jerk objection to nearly everything that was said or done. This time, though, something was different. I had chosen to sit in the back of the chapel so I could simply and freely observe. But instead of nitpicking and criticizing, I found myself contemplating questions that were slowly taking shape in my mind: "What if that man, the priest, is who they say he is? What if he is really doing what they say he is doing? What if what they say is happening is actually happening?" As I slowly considered these questions in the light of what I had learned from the Scriptures and early

Christian writings pertaining to the Real Presence of Christ in the Eucharist, I was left quite literally speechless—something which, for those who know me well, comes awfully close to a confirming miracle in my conversion to Catholicism!

After Mass, I had breakfast with Marcus Grodi and tried to share with him what had happened to me during Mass, but the words just stuck in my throat. Later in the day, I tried to relate my experience to Scott and Kimberly Hahn, but with the same results. That night, when I called home, I tried to explain it all to Gloria. Once again, the words would not come.

Please keep in mind that, as a Church of Christ preacher, this was all a bit difficult to swallow. We were schooled to be leery of subjective experiences. As a rule, we demanded cold, hard, objective facts with the accompanying "chapter and verse" from Scripture. Yet the Scriptures themselves testify to the marvelous ways in which God works in our hearts, ways that many might call subjective. Would I become a Catholic based merely upon a fuzzy, subjective, emotional experience? Hardly. And that is not what occurred that morning. What *did* occur was that God took all of the "cold, hard, objective facts" that I had learned concerning the Eucharist, tied them together, and removed my self-imposed barriers to understanding. In a word, He gave *grace*. And with that grace, I knew that one day I would be Catholic.

Chapter 9

# *The Home Stretch*

It was twelve days from the time of my return home from the *CHNetwork* retreat until Christmas Eve, 1993. When that holy night finally arrived, it was like no other I had ever experienced. The stars seemed brighter. The anticipation was greater. The presence of mystery was perceptible. I knew, even then, the reason: I was falling in love.

My nine years in the Church of Christ had conditioned me to exhibit a certain degree of reservation regarding Christmas. While celebrated as a family and cultural event, Christmas was rarely observed in any religious sense by members of the Churches of Christ because they don't see any instructions concerning such in the New Testament. Some extremists among them even go out of their way to make their point by not only avoiding any mention of Christ's birth during the month of December, but by singing traditional Christmas hymns in July. One elder I knew refused to observe Christmas because, in his words, it was "Romish," and to do so would, *ipso facto*, pay homage to the Roman Catholic Church.

With the graces I had received at Steubenville, however, my reservations were swallowed up by *wonder*. For the first time in years, I spent the Christmas season contemplating the ineffable mystery of our Lord's Incarnation. Such contemplation not only brought me closer to Christ but also instilled and nurtured within me a deep and abiding love for His Mother. The more I thought about the baby Jesus, the more I loved His Blessed Mother. As my love for Mary grew, so did my desire to please her divine Son.

The die was cast. There was no turning back. I knew that I would be Catholic. Yet it would be another fifteen months before my first Holy Communion would consummate my union with the Mystical Body of Christ in its fullest expression, the Catholic Church. While filled with intense anticipation, those fifteen months were to be tumultuous ones beset with struggles.

Within days of informing another preacher of my intentions, I received a call from a former instructor at the Sunset School of Preaching. He became so deeply concerned that in less than twenty-four hours, he appeared on my doorstep, which was no small feat considering that Lubbock, Texas, was more than 1,100 miles away. Our meeting was tense and emotional, but I will always appreciate the sincere charity he demonstrated in coming to see me.

Other preachers contacted me. Elders came to visit me. Friends expressed dismay. Family members voiced their concerns. All of them were sincere. Most were convinced that I would lose my eternal salvation and lead my family as well into damnation. Each of them demonstrated charity when they put their faith into action by reaching out to me in response to what they believed to be a catastrophe in the making, and I will always appreciate them for this.

More than one attempted to find a psychological reason for my "defection." My reasons, however, were not psychological: they were doctrinal and historical. Any psychological benefits I have received from becoming Catholic are attributable to the power of the truth and the therapeutic graces of the Sacraments.

More than one did their best to undermine the foundations of the Catholic faith in my mind. They failed to recognize that to undermine the foundations of the Catholic faith is to undercut the basis for the practice of Christianity in *any* form. As subsequent chapters of this book will underscore, to undermine the teaching authority of the Catholic Church is to despise the only means whereby any Christian can have infallible certitude concerning both the canon of Scripture and the authentic meaning of Scripture.

More than one expressed the opinion that I had fallen victim to the "strong delusion" spoken of by St. Paul in 2 Thessalonians 2:11-12. One went so far as to suggest that my allegedly deluded state was due to "flirtation with religious error." Yet, flirtation was not my pitfall. My pitfall, if indeed it was a pitfall, was to ask questions, and the questions I asked were legitimate questions. They were questions of such foundational significance as to require satisfying answers at all costs. They were questions that have found satisfying answers in—and only in—the Roman Catholic Church. They were questions pertaining to the issues addressed in the next two chapters.

# Part II

*The Primary Issue:*

*Authority*

# Chapter 10

# *Problems with a Restorationist Ecclesiology*

In my journey to the Catholic faith, two clearly related subjects stood in the forefront: ecclesiology (the study of the Church) and the Sacred Scriptures. They are related because one's understanding of the Church affects one's approach to the Scriptures and vice versa. Together, they can be logically grouped under the heading of *authority*. They will be considered separately in this chapter and the one that follows.

In regard to these two subjects, the Stone-Campbell Churches of Christ had presented me with an approach to Christianity that sought to use the "Bible *alone*" in order to "restore" the "New Testament Church," ostensibly making possible the elimination of denominational divisions. Embracing this vision of Christianity, I joined the Churches of Christ in 1985. Ironically, it would be the recognition of the shortcomings inherent in this "restorationist ecclesiology" and the problems intrinsic to a "Bible *alone*" approach to authority that would eventually result in my being received into the Catholic Church in 1995.

The Churches of Christ are not the only "restorationists" that have ever appeared on the religious landscape. The Puritans were restorationists, as were many Baptist denominations in their early days. In addition, our modern day has seen a proliferation of sects espousing many variations of restorationism. It could be said that virtually all non-Catholic traditions are "restorationists" in the sense that they all generally focus on one particular period in history as the Church's "golden age" to which we must return. Protestants tend to focus on the first century, Anglicans on the first four centuries, and Eastern Orthodox on the first eight centuries. Many of the proliferating modern independent Mega-churches insist that they are merely returning to the pristine Church of the second chapter of Acts. For all practical purposes, however, they all are claiming to "restore" the pure Gospel of the period to which they appeal.

Characteristic to all of them is an ecclesiology that depicts the Church as having departed from her purity of doctrine and practice soon after their respective "golden age" of choice. All of them purport to be bypassing centuries of doctrinal mutations by means of the "Bible *alone*" and thereby restoring the Church in accord with God's original design and intent. They all rely upon this idea of "apostasy" and "restoration" in order to justify their existence as a denomination separate from other denominations and, most importantly, their distinct existence apart from the Catholic Church.

The following excerpts from a popular Church of Christ tract are offered as an example:

> In the city of Jerusalem on the first Pentecost following His Ascension into heaven, Jesus Christ established the divine kingdom or church, the record of which is presented in the second chapter of Acts.[9]

> For several years following its beginning…the church continued as one united body by maintaining the purity of its divine pattern as set forth in the Scriptures; but with the passing of the years it gradually fell under the influence of false teachers and their erroneous doctrines, resulting in a general apostasy or falling away from the divine standard.[10]

At this point, one begins to encounter variations in the presentation. Some maintain that Christ always had a faithful remnant somewhere on the planet; others insist that the entire Church fell away completely only to be "restored" at some later point in history. Variations of the story notwithstanding, all who subscribe to restorationist theories are in agreement on one thing: the Church established by Jesus Christ experienced a massive falling away that lasted for well over a millennium.

The problem with such an accounting of Church history is simply that it is decidedly unscriptural. Just take a few moments to reflect on what the Scriptures say about the Church of Jesus Christ. More than five centuries before the birth of Christ, a prophecy was given that sets the stage for our expectations regarding the Messianic Kingdom:

> And in the days of those kings the God of heaven will set up a kingdom which shall never be destroyed, nor shall its sovereignty be left to another people. It shall break in pieces all these kingdoms and bring them to an end, and it shall stand forever (Daniel 2:44).

Earlier, within the context of this same prophecy, the kingdom of the Messiah was likened unto a stone that "became a great mountain and filled the whole earth" (Daniel 2:35). These words are universally recognized as being a prophecy concerning the Church. They create the expectation of a kingdom that would conquer, expand, and last forever! The New Testament writings offer us a picture of the Church that is in complete harmony with this prophecy of Daniel.

Consider the following treatment: Jesus said that His Kingdom was like a mustard seed that, when planted, grows into a large tree (Matthew 13:31-32). He spoke of its all-pervading influence by likening it unto leaven (Matthew 13:33). Our Lord declared to His apostles that He would build His Church and the gates of Hades would not prevail against it (Matthew 16:18). The apostle Paul refers to this same Church as being "the pillar and bulwark of the truth" (1 Timothy 3:15), the instrument by which God has chosen to make known His wisdom (Ephesians 3:10), and in which He will be glorified "to all generations" (Ephesians 3:12). Our Savior considered the unity of this Church, His Church, to be a vital testimony to the authenticity of His own mission (John 17:20-21). This fact is further emphasized by Jesus' final words before His Ascension: "You shall be My witnesses...to the end of the earth" (Acts 1:8). In Matthew's account of the same event, Jesus further assures His disciples with the familiar words, "Lo, I am with you always, to the close of the age" (Matthew 28:20).

Do these words of the Master sound like the description of a Kingdom that was destined to fail? Are we to believe that Christ worked so mightily with His Church in the first century, only to let it disappear from view for well over a thousand years? Yet this is exactly what a Restorationist Ecclesiology requires one to believe. From a Restorationist's point of view, the Lord simply utilized the Church to write a book, after which He, for all practical purposes, ceased to work in, through, and with the Church. Now I realize that few men, if any, would ever state the Restorationist position in such terms, but such is the *implication* of the position. As we have just seen, however, the Scriptures will not allow for such an idea.

At this point, some may be thinking about all the sobering warnings issued in the New Testament concerning false teachers and apostasy. Warnings about false teachers and apostasy, however, do not add up to a complete sinking of the ship. The warnings themselves do not require such an interpretation, and the verses we have already considered will not allow it. Christ's purpose for His Church could not and will not be thwarted by enemies from without or within.

Almost invariably, the warnings are relative to a specific concern identified in the context. For example, Jesus' warning about "false prophets, who come to you in sheep's clothing but inwardly are ravenous wolves" (Matthew 7:15) concerns those who would go against what He had just finished teaching in the Sermon on the

Mount. Peter's warning that "there will be false teachers among you, who will secretly bring in destructive heresies" (2 Peter 2:1) refers specifically to those who would promote immorality and go even so as far as "denying the Master who bought them." Once again, when John solemnly warned that "many false prophets have gone out into the world" (1 John 4:1), he had in mind those who would deny that Jesus had come in the flesh. Historically, these warnings found their fulfillment in the various Gnostic heresies. Finally, Paul's warning about "the man of lawlessness" and the "falling away" (2 Thessalonians 2:3 (KJV)) fits the description of the self-deifying Roman emperors and the falling away of many believers in the face of Roman persecution.

The point is that none of these warnings predict that the entire Church will become devastated and laid waste by false teachers. The writings of the early Fathers were, in large part, refutations of wild, heretical sects like the Gnostics—sects that fit the descriptions given in the Scriptural warnings concerning false teachers. However, they were simply that: *heretical* sects. The word *heresy* comes from a Greek word that denotes *an act of taking, selecting, or choosing.* In other words, these false teachers had *taken* from the true faith only that which they desired and *chosen* their own interpretations of the faith over the orthodox teachings of the Church. In so doing, they set themselves over and against the universal Church (the Catholic Church). The Greek word from which we derive the word *catholic* means *universal* (and, in a sense, *whole and entire*). Therefore, to even speak of heretics is, by implication, to acknowledge the existence of the main body from which they fell away.

Yes, the false teachers came and, yes, many believers fell away. Through it all, however, Christ's Church marched on, faithful to the One who supernaturally equips her for her divine mission. Such was the promise of our Lord; such is the testimony of history.

Furthermore, to advocate that Christ's Church completely fell away or became so severely weakened as to *essentially* vanish is to believe by implication that God left this planet without any real hope of salvation for more than a thousand years. Some claim that the Scriptures were always available to teach men the way of salvation, but the canon of Scripture was not settled until the fourth century. In addition, the printing press was not invented until A.D. 1450. Prior to that time, copies of the Scriptures were relatively scarce. For most of 1400 years, therefore, the world learned of salvation in Christ through the oral transmission of the Gospel message.

Please consider the words of St. Paul to the Athenians:

> The times of ignorance God overlooked, but now he commands all men everywhere to repent, because he has fixed a day on which he will judge the world in righteousness by a man whom he has appointed, and of this he has given assurance to all men by raising him from the dead (Acts 17:30-31).

In effect, St. Paul says, "No more excuses!" Why the apparent change in policy? Why won't ignorance be overlooked anymore? *Because light has come into the world!* The Kingdom of God and of His Christ has come and it was going to take the message of "repentance and forgiveness of sins" (Luke 24:47) to the entire world. This message would be delivered by messengers. Without a living, growing, faithful Church, however, the message would never have been proclaimed and every soul on the planet—*for more than a thousand years*—would have perished without having had the chance to hear the Gospel. Such a thought is not only incredible, it is obscene, because it is totally out of character with the Gospel. God's only-begotten Son did not suffer for the salvation of this world only to have His plans effectively halted by the frailties and failings of men.

Why then are such views of Church history, such as notions of complete apostasy, even entertained in the first place? The answer can be found in the widespread and arbitrary utilization of the Reformation principle of *sola Scriptura*. Using this dogma as a starting point, numerous men have formed a picture in their minds of what they think the Church ought to look like based upon their own, private interpretation of the Bible. Upon failing to find such a Church *anywhere* in the annals of history, they conclude that the Church of Christ underwent a complete and massive apostasy. They subsequently attempt to add credibility to this theory by referring to scriptural predictions of apostasy. If, however, as we have already seen, the Scriptures clearly teach that Christ's Church would be a dynamic, growing, and everlasting Kingdom, and if, as we have already seen, the scriptural predictions about apostasy do not refer to a complete falling away of the Lord's Church, why then don't the proponents of the "Great Apostasy" theory consider that maybe it is their own mental pictures of the Church that are flawed?

The undeniable fact is that the *only* Church to be found continuously throughout history is the Catholic Church.[*] Equally undeniable is the fact that the only place a modern day Stone-Campbell Church of Christ—or, for that matter, any present-day Protestant church—can be found prior to the sixteenth century is in the imaginations of those who read their particular churches into the Scriptures.

The writings of the first, second, and third century Christians reveal a Church that was distinctly Catholic in faith and practice. They believed in baptismal regeneration, Infant Baptism, the Real Presence of Christ in the Eucharist, the primacy of the bishop of Rome, the communion of saints, and Purgatory (see Appendix A for topically arranged citations from the Scriptures, the Catechism

---

[*] The Eastern Orthodox Churches can also claim an unbroken existence in one sense, but not in another. While they have valid apostolic succession going back to the Apostles, their separation from the unity of the Bishop of Rome (the pope) is not in harmony with their own practice during the first millennium of the Church. In that sense, their current status cannot be traced back to the beginnings of Christianity because their current posture towards the successor of St. Peter is out of harmony with their own beginnings.

of the Catholic Church, and the writings of the early Fathers in order to demonstrate the continuity of Catholic teaching from the earliest days of the Church to the present time.)

I mention these items in order to make the point that the Church did *not* mutate over the centuries into what is now the Catholic Church. If the notion of a "Great Apostasy" was true, then the Church, far from experiencing an insidiously imperceptible corruption, would have had to undergo a cataclysmic revolution before the ink on the last New Testament epistle barely had time to dry. To believe in the evil influence of false teachers is one thing, but to believe that they so quickly seduced the entire Church into total apostasy is another thing altogether. The Scriptures do not teach such, nor even *allow* it.

In summary, one of the major reasons I could not remain a member of the Stone-Campbell Churches of Christ or, for that matter, a Protestant of any stripe, was due to major problems inherent in their ecclesiologies. While the Scriptures do warn about false prophets and apostasy, they also clearly teach that Christ's Church will never be destroyed. These same Scriptures present a Church that is a visible, identifiable institution with a visible, identifiable hierarchy. In addition, the earliest Christian writings all testify to a Church that is distinctly Catholic in its faith and practice. Furthermore, to subscribe to the notion of the "Great Apostasy" is to deny the essential nature, mission, protection, and glory given by God to His Church as revealed in Sacred Scripture. Consequently, I was forced to conclude that a Restorationist Ecclesiology is contrary to the truths of Scripture, the facts of history, and sound reason.

> And in the days of those kings the God of heaven will set up a kingdom which shall never be destroyed, nor shall its sovereignty be left to another people. It shall break in pieces all these kingdoms and bring them to an end, and it shall stand forever (Daniel 2:44).

Chapter 11

# *Problems with* Sola Scriptura

As I sat across from a young man called Johnny*, I could sense both his certitude and his perplexity. A young and recent convert to the Churches of Christ, he was so strong in his doctrinal convictions that he had all the confidence of a young lion stalking his quarry. He was noticeably baffled, though, by my failure to concede certain points that, in his mind, were quite obvious and unassailable. Finally, in exasperation, he held up his Bible and exclaimed, "Look, if everyone just went by the clear teachings of this book, there wouldn't be any religious divisions!"

The issue of authority is the primary issue that divides Catholics and non-Catholics. This division does not consist in questioning the authority of the Word of God proper, but in defining what constitutes the Word of God and *how* we are to accurately understand it.

Both Catholics and Protestants believe that they are standing firmly upon the revealed will of God. The Protestant, however, believes that such revelation is contained solely in the Scriptures, whereas the Catholic believes that God's revelation is contained in the Church's *deposit of faith* that includes both Sacred Scripture and Sacred Tradition. In Jude 3, for example, we read:

> Beloved, being very eager to write to you of our common salvation, I found it necessary to write appealing to you to contend for the faith which was once for all delivered to the saints (Jude 1:3).

Here the author presumes upon the common knowledge of a previously delivered *deposit of faith*.

Reading Karl Keating's *Catholicism and Fundamentalism* provoked me to reconsider the underlying assumption pertaining to authority and my *modus operandi* as a Church of Christ preacher. This same underlying assumption is at the heart of virtually all of Protestantism, namely, *sola Scriptura*. Protestantism typically espouses an approach to religious authority that views the Bible as completely sufficient *in and of itself* (*formal* sufficiency). That is to say, most Protestants consider the Bible to be self-authenticating, self-explanatory, and the sum total of God's revealed will.

Catholics, on the other hand, believe in the *material sufficiency* of the Scriptures. They affirm that every dogma of the Catholic faith is contained at least *implicitly*—if not explicitly—in the Bible. In other words, the content of the faith is demonstrable in the Scriptures. Catholics do not consider the Scriptures to be *formally sufficient* because a living, teaching office (the Magisterium of the Church) is required to set forth authentic interpretations and applications of the Bible's meaning (or else the Bible is subject to misunderstanding and distortion).

Furthermore, it is the oral, living Tradition of the Church—handed down from the Apostles—that serves as the context in which the Scriptures are studied and their authentic meanings ascertained. Admittedly, non-Catholics, often without realizing it, have fundamentally the same view. This is why, for example, Protestants don't simply distribute Bibles *alone*. Instead they send out missionaries and evangelists as "qualified" teachers to ensure that converts come to the "correct" interpretation of the Scriptures.

In this chapter, we will examine the problems inherent in a *sola Scriptura* approach to authority by examining the propensity of Protestants to proffer "biblical objections" to the Catholic faith.

As noted in our look at the problems with a Restorationist Ecclesiology, the Protestant notion of the "Great Apostasy" derives in part from the existence of certain *perceived* discrepancies between the Bible and the Catholic faith. Armed with these presumably incriminating "biblical objections," proponents of the "Great Apostasy" then proceed to lambaste the "apostate" Catholic Church. What assumptions, however, underlie these supposed biblical objections?

Make no mistake that those who would launch a "scriptural" assault on the Catholic Church do so based upon at least three major assumptions: A self-evident canon of Scripture, the *perspicuity* of Scripture, and *sola Scriptura.* Before examining these three assumptions, however, let us take a moment to visualize what it is we are considering.

Picture, if you will, all the alleged "biblical objections" to the Catholic faith. Imagine them being placed upon a table. This particular table is a three-legged table. The fact that this table has only three legs is not a problem, provided that all three legs possess integrity. In this illustration, the three legs represent the three assumptions mentioned above that underlie *all* biblical objections to the Catholic faith. The question is, will all three legs hold up under examination? If just one of the legs fails, the entire table collapses and with it the "biblical objections" to the Catholic faith. As we shall soon see, all three legs fail to pass the threefold test of history, reason, and Scripture.

The first assumption is that of a self-evident canon of Scripture. The word *canon* comes from a Greek word meaning "cane" or "reed" signifying an instrument of measurement—a standard. Over time, the word came to have the meaning of "catalogue" or "list." This is the sense in which it is used here: the canon—or *list*—of Sacred Writings. In other words, the canon of Scripture refers to the list of books that are to be included in the Bible.

Yet how can one know with certainty what writings from antiquity are to be regarded as Sacred Scripture?

Correspondingly, if no such certainty can be found outside the Catholic Church, is it legitimate to oppose the Catholic faith by employing supposedly biblical objections? In that case, the non-Catholic finds himself in the unenviable position of opposing the Catholic Church by appealing to the Bible, which relies on the Catholic Church's teaching authority for its authentication.

This is one of the most troubling of all doctrinal dilemmas for the non-Catholic, because the New Testament writings were not delivered to the Church in the neatly bound package we have today. In addition to the twenty-seven books of our present New Testament canon, there were dozens of other writings in circulation that claimed apostolic origins. History bears testimony that the early Church, while having a uniform faith and practice—or Tradition—lacked a consensus as to which writings should be included in the New Testament canon of Scripture. Some churches accepted certain writings as canonical that were later rejected, such as the *Didache* or the *First Letter of Clement*; other churches rejected writings that were later accepted as canonical, such as *Third John* or *Revelation*. It was not until A.D. 367, with the 39th Festal Letter of St. Athanasius, that the canon of the twenty-seven books we now recognize was set forth in its entirety. The Council of Hippo (393) and the Council of Carthage (397)—both of which were local councils of Catholic bishops—were the first Church councils to list our present day canon of New Testament writings in its entirety.

These facts are admitted, though often in cautionary language, by non-Catholic biblical scholars. Norman L. Geisler and William E. Nix, for example, in their popular book, *A General Introduction to the Bible*, admit that there was not a universal, uniform canon until the latter half of the fourth century.[12] F.W. Mattox (former President of Lubbock Christian College—a Church of Christ institution) made the amazing admission, in his work entitled *The Eternal Kingdom*, that the New Testament canon was unsettled in the second century, making oral transmission the primary means of handing down Christian doctrine. This, he concluded, contributed to the rapid spread of false ideas. This invites the question that if God intended His Church to be guided by the Bible *alone*, how is it that He made no provision for an established New Testament canon prior to the fourth century?

These historical facts prove most damaging to the "Bible *only*" position. The absence of a uniform canon of New Testament Scripture demands the conclusion that the early Christians could *not* have been "Bible *only*" Christians. How could they have been when they could *not* agree on which writings were inspired? History shows, however, that they did share a common standard of authority, which was the deposit of faith delivered to, and explicated by, the Church. Therefore, while the settling of the canon issue was indeed an important one, it was *not* a "life and death" matter for the apostolic Church. For three centuries of amazing apostolic zeal and missionary expansion, the Church continued fully functional even though she lacked a uniform NT canon. This issue, however, is one of absolute importance for those who subscribe to a *sola Scriptura* approach to authority.

Also, in view of the historical facts and considering the absence of an inspired table of contents, it is impossible to know with any degree of certainty what the authentic canon of New Testament Scripture is apart from the teaching authority of the Catholic Church. This is crucial, because the necessity of certitude regarding the canon is hard to overstate. A *fallible* collection of infallible writings is essentially worthless because it admits the possibility of the omission of authentic writings or the inclusion of uninspired writings. This fact alone should provoke some serious discomfort in those who seek to justify a "Bible *only*" position.

The simple fact is that the Scriptures themselves offer little if any assistance in determining the canon. History gives us many mixed signals. Reason alone cannot settle the matter.

The only means we have by which we can know with certainty which books comprise the divinely inspired canon of the New Testament Scriptures is the authoritative testimony of the early Church...and *that* Church was distinctly Catholic. Even a cursory reading of the earliest Christian writings reveals a Church that was distinctly Catholic in faith and practice, with a hierarchy of bishops, priests, and deacons, that believed they partook of the literal Body and Blood of Christ in the Eucharist, that believed in baptismal regeneration, and practiced Infant Baptism. The canon of Scripture is by no means self-evident. It can be determined *only* by consulting a reliable authority external to itself—and what other authority can that be except the Catholic Church?

I once discussed this matter with a particularly fervent Church of Christ preacher who indignantly retorted, "God's Word does not need authentication by man!" While that response may make for a great sermon line, it hardly addresses the issue. The canon of Scripture simply is *not* revealed in Scripture. Therefore, it is necessary to consult an authority *outside* of Scripture to derive the canon. Moreover, in order for the canon to be reliable, it must be infallible, but in order to have an infallible canon, the source from which the canon is derived must itself be infallible. It is necessary, therefore, to ascribe infallible teaching authority to the Catholic Church if one is to regard her pronouncements on the canon of Scripture as infallible. There is no middle ground. Consequently, the first leg of our three-legged table offers no support whatsoever to those who would amass "biblical objections" to the Catholic faith.

The second assumption to examine is the *perspicuity* of the Scriptures, or the idea that the Scriptures are so clear that they are *self-explanatory,* a necessary fundamental assumption underlying *sola Scriptura.* In order for *sola Scriptura* to be functional, the Scriptures *must* be shown to be perspicuous.

For this, we must answer the question of how we can be certain of the accuracy of our personal, private interpretations of the Scriptures? If absolute certainty is not possible, is it legitimate to assail the Catholic Church with "biblical objections" when these are based upon private, potentially faulty interpretations? In order for such polemical onslaughts to be legitimate, it must first be demonstrated that the Scriptures, separate and apart from Sacred Tradition and the teaching authority of the Church, are clear and self-explanatory. Such, however, is not the case.

Historically, we can see glaring problems with the notion that the Scriptures are perspicuous. Instead of furthering the Kingdom of God, the Reformation battle cry of *"sola Scriptura"* has resulted in literally thousands of competing denominations—and no end is in sight. Some have even reported that the past few decades have witnessed the creation of 200 to 300 new denominations per year! The Stone-Campbell Restoration Movement, with its plea to "speak where the Bible speaks," has not fared much better. With every new attempt to unify the movement, new divisions are spawned precisely because of the inability of even noble-minded individuals to agree on the meaning of Scripture. How can this be if sincere and searching souls are all studying the same, presumably clear book?

Some have attempted to address this difficulty by suggesting that truly sincere and searching individuals will come to agreement on the essentials of the faith. But who decides what are the essentials? Such a determination is a matter of private interpretation and is the basis for most, if not all, religious division. For example, within the Stone-Campbell Movement, which was initially a unity movement, brethren are seriously divided on numerous issues ranging from the use of multiple communion cups to the wearing of head coverings by women. If these disagreements involve "non-essentials," why is there division? If the disagreeing parties are composed of sincere individuals, why can't they come to agreement based upon the supposedly clear teachings of the Bible? The fact is that there are numerous areas in which the Scriptures are not as clear as non-Catholics would like them to be.

All of this should come as no surprise, for it is contrary to sound reason to expect a written document to be the *sole* basis for the governing of *any* group of people, religious or secular. Our own nation has its written Constitution, but it also has the Supreme Court to settle disputes as to what the Constitution actually means. Utter chaos would result if Americans were simply issued copies of the Constitution and told to live by their personal, private interpretations. Yet that is basically how non-Catholics view the Bible. Surely God knew the anarchy that would follow such a course; surely He made provisions to prevent such. Indeed, we find that He has done exactly that in giving us the Church, "the pillar and bulwark of the truth" (1 Timothy 3:15).

Furthermore, the Scriptures themselves testify to the fact that they can be somewhat less than clear and subject to misunderstanding. The apostle Peter warned his readers that the Scriptures were subject to distortion by the "ignorant and unstable" (2 Peter 3:14-16). The necessity of prior, authentic teaching for the proper understanding of the Scriptures is implicit in this apostolic warning. Ironically, the mere existence of every Protestant seminary and Church of Christ school of preaching is a tacit acknowledgement of this reality (this will be addressed more fully in Chapter 13).

So we must ask by whom are we to be taught? If, as Peter implies, the Scriptures require prior knowledge in order to be accurately understood, who outside the apostolic Catholic Church is capable of providing that knowledge? Absolutely nobody begins building from *scratch*. All Bible students begin with certain foundational suppositions that provide the framework around which they systematize what they assimilate from the Scriptures. The crucial question then is whether or not these foundational suppositions are sound, because unsound starting suppositions lead to unsound conclusions.

It would appear that the second leg of our table, the perspicuity of Scripture, lacks integrity. It fails to pass the threefold examination of history, reason, and Scripture. Our table now has only one remaining leg—that of *sola Scriptura* or the Bible *only*.

Historically, the supposition of *sola Scriptura* can be shown to have originated during the time of the sixteenth century Protestant Reformation. Prior to this time, the Scriptures were revered as being a priceless part of, and a reflection of, the deposit of faith. In addition, it had been universally recognized throughout Christendom that the role of providing for the authentic understanding and application of the Scriptures was entrusted to the divinely ordained teaching authority of the Church. As we have already seen, the notion that the early Church was comprised of "Bible *only*" Christians is baseless due to the fact that they lacked a uniform canon until the fourth century.

Suppose, for the sake of argument, that there were "Bible *only*" Christians in the early centuries of the Church. Where were they? Why didn't they reform the "apostate" Church? For that matter, why didn't they simply "nip it in the bud"? Remember, they lived in apostolic times, the faith was delivered in their cultural setting, and the Scriptures were written in their native tongue. They would be more in touch with the apostolic faith than *any* group of "Bible *only*" Christians living nearly 2,000 years later. How is it, then, that they disappeared from the scene without a trace? There is only one plausible answer: *They never existed.* Again, there was not a uniform canon of Scripture until the fourth century, and it was nearly a thousand years after that before the first "Bible *only*" Christians appeared on the scene.

An unavoidable conundrum arises with the notion of *sola Scriptura:* if *sola Scriptura* is a sound principle, then it should be clearly enunciated as such in the Scriptures. But where does the Bible teach the doctrine of *sola Scriptura?* Correspondingly, how can s*ola Scriptura* be true if the Bible alone does not teach it? As we shall see, not only is *sola Scriptura* not taught within the pages of Sacred Scripture, quite the opposite is true.

In seeking to justify their position, proponents of *sola Scriptura* unleash a flood of Scripture references, all of which supposedly prove their doctrine. *None* of the verses, however, *in their context*, set forth or support the notion of *sola Scriptura*. It is beyond the scope of this book to examine every one of these references, so instead, we will briefly consider four passages that are often quoted in defense of a "Bible *only*" approach to authority.

Beginning in the Gospels, most proponents of *sola Scriptura* are quick to point out Jesus' presumed disdain for *tradition*:

> And why do you transgress the commandment of God for the sake of your tradition? For God commanded, 'Honor your father and your mother,' and, 'He who speaks evil of father or mother, let him surely die.' But you say, 'If anyone tells his father or his mother, What you would have gained from me is given to God, he need not honor his father.' So, for the sake of your tradition, you have made void the word of God (Matthew 15:3-6).

Notice, however, that Jesus is not speaking of tradition in the Catholic sense of the word. The word tradition means simply "that which is handed down." When used by Catholics in reference to the Christian faith, it refers to that which has been handed down to the Church by Christ through the Apostles. This deposit of faith (Tradition) includes, but is not limited to, the Sacred Scriptures. Jesus never wrote anything, nor did He tell His disciples to do so. Instead, He promised to be with them (and, correspondingly, the Church) until the end of time and to guide them by the Holy Spirit. He commissioned them to *preach* the Good News to every creature, and that is what they did.

In the Gospels, Jesus condemns the *traditions of men* if and only when they supplant or obscure the commandments of God.

The Sacred Tradition of the Church, however, far from being the mere traditions of men, is the Christian faith itself as delivered by the apostles to their successors, the bishops.* Furthermore, the fact that Jesus *specified* the "traditions of men" indicates that He was not referring to *all* traditions. He did not deny the existence of tradition that was divine in origin. Hence the apostle Paul, by inspiration of the Holy Spirit, could admonish the Christians at Thessalonica to, "stand firm and hold to the traditions which you were taught by us, either by word of mouth or by letter" (2 Thessalonians 2:15). It is, in fact, only because of the Church's Sacred Tradition that "Bible *only*" Christians even have a Bible from which to quote.

Moving on to the book of Acts, advocates of *sola Scriptura* often quote from Luke's comments concerning the Bereans:

> They received the word with all eagerness, examining the Scriptures daily to see if these things were so (Acts 17:11).

These words do anything *but* prove *sola Scriptura.* The message preached by Paul and Silas to the Jews in Berea had not yet been penned in Scripture—it was an *oral* message. The searching of the Scriptures by the Bereans referred to their examination of the *Old Testament* prophetical texts undoubtedly referred to by Paul in his apostolic preaching. Their searching of the Old Testament Scriptures was commended because it demonstrated their

---

* Most non-Catholics do not believe that bishops are the successors of the Apostles. They often will insist that the bishops, in order to be the successors of the Apostles, must perform miraculous signs just like the Twelve. However, the bishops are not successors of the Apostles in the sense of having to lay again the foundation of the Church—such has been completed, and for such were the miracles granted. Rather, Catholic bishops are successors to the Apostles in the sense that they fulfill the duties entailed by the apostolically ordained *office of overseers*. The Apostles themselves appointed overseers (bishops) in all the churches to govern the faithful in their absence, to safeguard the deposit of faith, and to administer the sacraments. This is what the bishops of the Catholic Church have done for nearly 2,000 years.

openness to the truth. However, this searching of the Scriptures was not done for the Church's sake. Rather, they did so for the purpose of convincing *themselves* of Jesus' Messianic mission. In other words, St. Paul presented Jesus Christ as the fulfillment of Old Testament prophecy. The Jews at Berea looked at those prophecies in order to see if what St. Paul was saying was true. In so doing, they saw that Jesus did indeed fulfill the Old Testament Scriptures.

Suppose that the Bereans had come back the next day and said, "Wait a minute, Paul, we read the scroll of Isaiah last night and we disagree with your interpretation." Would Paul have been forced to reconsider the teachings he had personally received from Jesus Christ in the light of the "Bible *alone*"? That would be ludicrous. These verses, therefore, have *nothing* to offer in defense of the doctrine of *sola Scriptura*.

Some advocates of *sola Scriptura* insist that the following admonition of St. Paul to the Corinthians supports their position:

> I have applied all this to myself and Apollos for your benefit, brethren, that you may learn by us not to go beyond what is written, that none of you may be puffed up in favor of one against another (1 Corinthians 4:6).

At first glance, Paul's directive to "not go beyond what is written" appears to be an endorsement of *sola Scriptura*. However, any attempt to squeeze such an interpretation into the historical context of this verse creates some serious problems. First, nearly all New Testament references to "Scripture" refer to the writings of the Old Testament. But Paul certainly did not intend to restrict the Corinthians to the Old Testament, or else they would have to ignore those writings that would later come to be recognized as the Scriptures of the New Testament—including the letter Paul had just written to them.

Second, Paul could not be restricting the Corinthians to the writings of the New Testament for at least two reasons. The canon of the New Testament was not yet complete (for example, Paul's *second* letter to the Corinthians was yet to be written). And for Paul to have so restricted his readers would have amounted to talking out of both sides of his mouth. Remember, in his Second Letter to the Thessalonians, Paul told the brethren to "hold to the traditions which you were taught, whether by word of mouth or by letter from us." These words of the apostle place oral tradition and written tradition on equal footing. First Corinthians 4:6, therefore, fails to offer any undisputable support to those seeking to prove *sola Scriptura.*

In this context, Paul was calling on the Corinthians to discard the inflated views they had of Apollos, Cephas (Peter), and Paul himself. In the course of this admonition, he quotes from several appropriate verses of Old Testament Scripture (cf. 1 Cor.1:19, 31; 3:19-20). Therefore, when he gets to chapter four, verse six, he is calling upon them to "not exceed what is written" (that is, to keep within the boundaries of the teachings set out for them in the verses of Old Testament Scripture that he had just finished quoting for them).

Finally, the *primary* text employed by the proponents of *sola Scriptura* is one addressed by St. Paul to his beloved son in the faith, St. Timothy:

> But as for you, continue in what you have learned and have firmly believed, knowing from whom you learned it and how from childhood you have been acquainted with the sacred writings which are able to instruct you for salvation through faith in Christ Jesus. All scripture is inspired by God and profitable for teaching, for reproof, for correction, and for training in righteousness, that the man of God may be complete, equipped for every good work (2 Timothy 3:14-17).

It has been said that if this passage proves *sola Scriptura*, it proves too much! Why? Because the Scriptures that Paul apparently had in mind were the Scriptures of the Old Testament, which were the only Scriptures that Timothy would have known "since childhood." The Old Testament Scriptures do indeed "instruct [one] for salvation" in Christ through the principles, typology, and prophecies that they contain—hence the reliance of apostolic preaching upon the Scriptures of the Old Testament. Who, though, would argue that one needs only the Old Testament Scriptures in order to be a fully equipped Christian? Also, please note what Paul *did* say and what he *did not* say. He *did* say that if our goal is to be fully equipped men of God, the Scriptures are *profitable* toward that goal. He did *not* say that the Scriptures *alone* are *sufficient* for the attaining of that goal. To help differentiate between "profitability" and "sufficiency," think of a soldier preparing for battle. Following the training manual for battle strategies would certainly prove profitable, but it would be far from *sufficient* in and of itself (a soldier also needs to get up off his duff and train physically).

If Paul had meant that Scripture alone was sufficient, he would have been inconsistent in his arguments. Consider his words in the previous chapter of that same letter:

> And what you have heard from me before many witnesses entrust to faithful men who will be able to teach others also (2 Timothy 2:2).

Note that it is the message that Timothy had *heard* from Paul that he was to pass on to faithful men who were to pass it on to still others *ad infinitum.* Let us also note that Paul apparently did not share the same trepidation about orally transmitted revelation that typically characterizes Protestantism. On the contrary, he seemed to have great confidence in God's ability to safeguard the message. This is seen in 2 Timothy 1:13-14, where Paul calls upon Timothy to guard through the Holy Spirit the treasure that had been entrusted to him. That treasure was the "pattern of sound words" he had "*heard*" from Paul, the oral deposit of faith.

None of the verses we have examined, which are the ones most commonly employed, offer any support for the Reformation invention of *sola Scriptura*. It does no good to claim that they set forth a "principle." How can *ten thousand* verses, linked together, be construed as teaching a principle that none of them teaches in its individual context? The fact is that *sola Scriptura* is not elucidated *anywhere* in the Scriptures. Ironically, it is an *unbiblical* doctrine.

As we look back at our three-legged table, what do we see? Not just one, but *all three* legs have collapsed under the weight of history, reason, and the Scriptures, and with them, all the so-called "biblical objections" to the Catholic faith.

What am I saying? Am I saying that the Scriptures are not the divinely inspired Word of God? *God forbid!* The Church is established on the sure foundation of God's Word. That revealed Word has come to us most definitively in Jesus Christ, *the Word made flesh.* His message has come down to us through His apostles, who *preached* that message and delivered it *orally* to those who were appointed to succeed them as bishops of the Church. Much of the apostolic message was committed to writing, but there is no indication in the Scriptures themselves that Christ ever intended that His followers would be guided *solely* by the Scriptures, much less by private interpretation of them. In fact, the nature of the Scriptures themselves leads us to quite the opposite conclusion. They were written *by* members of the Church *to* members of the Church regarding subject matter of importance to the Church.

Furthermore, each New Testament epistle presumed upon a body of shared knowledge between the writer and the recipients. When St. Paul opened his first letter to the Corinthians by saying, "Paul, called as an apostle of Jesus Christ," he did not have to insert a footnote introducing his readers to Jesus Christ because they already possessed the faith. They shared a common body of knowledge called the "deposit of Faith." That deposit of faith was presumed by St. Paul when he wrote. It was also relied upon by his recipients when they read what he wrote. In this way, written teaching simply built upon the existing oral teaching—the oral teaching forming the foundation for the written teaching. They went hand in hand, and the proper understanding of the written teaching required the prior knowledge provided by the oral teaching. This reality is alluded to by St. Peter when he speaks of the "untaught" distorting the Scriptures (2 Peter 3:14-16).

That body of shared, common knowledge is what we find in the *Sacred Tradition* of the Catholic Church. That this Tradition has been faithfully transmitted through the centuries is seen in the remarkable continuity of Catholic teaching from the earliest days of the Church until the present time. We should expect no less, for the Lord Himself promised to be with His Church, *"always, even to the end of the age."*

Bruce & Gloria with their five children. Front row (from left to right): Michael, Therese, and David. Back row (from left to right): Emily, Gloria, Bruce, and Mary.

# Part III

*What I Found in the*

*Catholic Church*

Chapter 12

# Christ in His Fullness

*There is one body and one Spirit, just as you were called
to the one hope that belongs to your call, one Lord, one
faith, one baptism, one God and Father of us all, who
is above all and through all and in all...And His gifts
were that some should be apostles, some prophets, some
evangelists, some pastors and teachers, to equip the
saints for the work of ministry, for building up the body
of Christ, until we all attain to the unity of the faith and
of the knowledge of the Son of God, to mature manhood,
to the measure of the stature of the fullness of Christ
(Ephesians 4:4-6, 11-13).*

In the introduction to this book, I referred to an exchange I
once had with a co-worker I called Joe*. Upon learning that
I was a convert to the Catholic faith, he asked, "What did you
find in Catholicism that you did not find in Protestantism?" After
years of reflecting on that question, I have been able to reduce
my answer to four words: Christ in His fullness. This is not to say
that I had not found Christ as a Protestant, because I had. But the
emphasis now is upon Christ in His *fullness.*

Our society is driven by the endless quest for personal
fulfillment. For most, this quest seems to have taken a wrong turn
somewhere along the way and degenerated into the superficial
pursuit of pleasure and the never-ending acquisition of material
wealth. Against this trend, however, the Gospel enlightens us to

the truth that the key to personal fulfillment, both now and in eternity, is *the fullness of Christ*. To have the fullness of Christ we must receive the fullness of the gifts that He desires to give us, which He entrusted to the Church. These gifts include, among others, the fullness of Christ's teaching and the fullness of Christ's sacraments.

Without exception, *every* Christian denomination and sect can be traced back to its ultimate origins in the Catholic Church. Even the Stone-Campbell Churches of Christ—which claim to be "non-denominational"—cannot escape their links to the Catholic Church through the former denominational affiliations of the founders of their movement. Whenever a group of Christians has broken away from the Catholic Church, it has in the process rejected some portion of the gifts that Christ desires all Christians to possess. It may be a teaching or several teachings; it may be a sacrament or several sacraments. Though obviously not intended, the result is the forfeiture of some aspect of the fullness of Christ as experienced in the historic Catholic Church.

It must be acknowledged that *none* of the gifts that Christ has given to His Church are superfluous. They have all been deposited with the Church for a reason. To be without any one of them is to be deprived of some avenue of grace that our Lord has provided in order to enable us to grow in the spiritual life and attain our ultimate union with Him in heaven. Is it possible to reach heaven without the full complement of the means of grace? The short answer is *yes*. But by way of imperfect analogy, it is like asking if one must have a full complement of supplies in order to make an arduous journey across the desert. While one could argue that water is more necessary than food and food more necessary than shoes, who would consider any of these three to be merely *optional?* Moreover, there is more to be considered regarding our eternal union with God than simply "making it" into heaven.

St. Paul, for example, clearly taught that rewards in heaven will differ according to how one builds upon the foundation of Christ in this life (1 Corinthians 3:10-15). Our Lord himself exhorts us to "lay up for yourselves treasures in heaven" (Matthew 6:19-20). The implication is that some in heaven will have greater rewards and more treasure than others in heaven. Since envy will have no place in heaven, this will not lead to resentment or bitterness. Nonetheless, the implication is that our progress in the spiritual life here on earth will have a direct impact on our experience of heaven in eternity. It, therefore, behooves the Christian to strive for that *perfection* of which Christ spoke in Matthew 5:48.* This perfection is possible only if we make *full* use of the *full* complement of gifts that Christ has given to the Church. It is only then that God's grace can have its *full* effect in our lives.

> For this reason I bow my knees before the Father, from whom every family in heaven and on earth is named, that according to the riches of His glory He may grant you to be strengthened with might through His Spirit in the inner man, and that Christ may dwell in your hearts through faith; that you, being rooted and grounded in love, may have power to comprehend with all the saints what is the breadth and length and height and depth, and to know the love of Christ which surpasses knowledge, that you may be filled with all the fullness of God (Ephesians 3:14-19).

* The word translated "perfect" in this text is the Greek word *teleios*. It is a *functional* term that does not refer to abstract or metaphysical perfection. For something to be "perfect" in the functional sense suggests that the object must fully realize the purpose for which it has been produced. For Christians, it means that we strive to cooperate with God's grace and thereby develop our full, unique potential in Christ (i.e. what St. Paul referred to as *"the measure of the stature of the fullness of Christ"* in the passage from Ephesians cited at the beginning of this chapter). For a more complete treatment of this concept, I recommend Father Ray Ryland's essay, "Does Being Catholic Make a Difference?" (*This Rock*, May 1995, available at www.catholic.com)

Chapter 13

# *Christ in the Fullness of His Word*

*If you continue in My word, you are truly My disciples, and you will know the truth, and the truth will make you free (John 8:31-32).*

The conversation had begun with a discussion of our common interest in the pro-life movement. When Tom* learned that I was Catholic, however, the conversation took a sharp turn. Eager to share with me the "true" Gospel, as he understood it, he proceeded to evangelize me. We stood in the hotel parking lot for more than an hour, deliberating our doctrinal differences. Noticeably agitated, he finally blurted out, "You think that your Church has all the truth!"

From the earliest days of the Protestant Reformation to the frontier preaching of Alexander Campbell and up into the modern era, there have been men who have, with all sincerity of conviction, proclaimed the Scriptures as the all-sufficient guide for matters pertaining to the Christian faith. In all earnestness, they have proposed that if Christians would but adhere to the "clear" and "essential" teachings of Scripture, strife among Christians would cease and Christian unity would be attained. As we saw in Chapter 11, however, the assumptions underlying a "Bible *only*" approach to authority are seriously flawed. Good men—honest and learned men—find themselves unable to agree on the list of essentials, much less upon their meaning and practical expressions. This shows that we need more than just the *text* of the infallible written Word of God. We must also have an infallible *understanding* of that Word if the faith is to be practiced with certitude and in unity with other believers.

For many Protestant Christians, the idea that one should seek, much less claim to have, an *infallible* understanding of God's Word is outlandish, presumptuous, and exceedingly arrogant. *Infallible,* however, simply means "to be without error." Surely our Blessed Lord—who *is* the Truth—wants us to have an error-free understanding of the truths pertaining to our salvation. So how can we desire anything less? And correspondingly, how could God not have made provision for such? Isn't it possible to have Christ in the *fullness* of His Word?

All Christians long for the fullness of God's Word. All ministers strive to present that fullness through their teaching. As a Church of Christ preacher, however, the best that I could do was to stand before the congregation and say, "Thus saith the Lord...*I think*," for it is impossible to have infallible certitude regarding the canon of Scripture separate and apart from the teaching authority of the Catholic Church. Therefore, as one who explicitly rejected that teaching authority, I had no basis for confidently asserting that the texts from which I preached were canonical. I *thought* them to be the Word of God, but I could not substantiate that belief in a convincing manner. Even if, for the sake of argument, canonical certitude was granted, by rejecting any form of ecclesiastical authority and in denying the veracity of the historic Catholic understanding of Scripture I could offer nothing more than my personal opinions as to the *meaning* of Scripture. I could present only what I *thought* to be solid explications of what I *thought* to be the Word of God. Hence, "Thus saith the Lord...*I think*."

Ironically, I often denied that my interpretations of Scripture were *interpretations*. Like many preachers, I considered my expositions of Scripture to be nothing more or less than an unfolding of its clear and obvious meaning. In this vein, I can well remember a homiletic device frequently employed by one of my instructors at the Sunset School of Preaching. Upon making a point in class, he would often exclaim, "That's not a matter of *interpretation!* It is simply a *quotation* of the Divine *Revelation* that was given by *inspiration!*" At the time, I found this rhythmic exclamation on the part of my instructor to be both invigorating and affirming. But as the years passed, I came to see it as being rather hollow. If, as his words implied, the meaning of Scripture is so self-evidently plain as to require no "interpretation," why have a school of preaching? In fact, why have teachers at all? If the Scriptures are indeed perspicuous, each individual should be able to simply read the Scriptures and put into practice the plenitude of obvious truths they contain. But as history has clearly demonstrated, such an approach to Sacred Scripture results in chaos and anarchy.

The fact of the matter is that all Christian communions *implicitly* recognize that the meaning of Scripture is often not as plain as many well-meaning preachers like to think. For this reason they do not simply distribute copies of Scripture without commentary. Every organization of which I am aware that distributes copies of Scripture invariably distributes *more* than the biblical text. Either the Bibles that they distribute contain instructions pertaining to how one receives salvation, or they distribute study materials along with the Bibles. In either case, such instructions and study materials are all based upon the official interpretations and beliefs of the distributing organization. Hence, even then, they implicitly acknowledge that proper understanding of the Bible requires instruction and guidance, which is the point made by St. Peter in 2 Peter 3:16 when he refers to the "untaught" who "distort" the Scriptures.

All denominations send out missionaries, teachers, and preachers who are deemed *qualified* to present the official scriptural interpretation of their respective groups. This is, in reality, a tacit admission that they do not have a "Bible *only*" *modus operandi* in the absolute sense, for they obviously recognize that the Scriptures are subject to distortion and misunderstanding. Accordingly, they emphasize the need for qualified teachers who will guide people to a "proper" understanding (that is, *their* understanding) of the Word.

Additionally, in every communion of Christians, from the smallest "house churches" to the largest denominations, there is some mechanism in place for the settling of doctrinal disputes. It may be a simple majority consensus; it may be the local board of elders; it may be a tribunal established at the denominational headquarters. Whatever form it takes, every communion of Christians has *some* form of "magisterial authority." Magisterial authority refers to the teaching office of the Church. In the Catholic Church, the Magisterium consists of the successor of St. Peter (the Pope) and the bishops in union with him. If anyone doubts that even fundamentalists and Churches of Christ have a magisterium, they have only to seek out and speak with a preacher who has been dismissed by his local "magisterium" for being doctrinally "unsound."

All of this gives voice to what few Protestant Christians seem to recognize or are prepared to admit, namely that all Christian communions operate with the same model of authority that is employed by the Roman Catholic Church: a triad of Scripture, Tradition, and Magisterium (see Appendix I for a fuller treatment of the subject of Sacred Tradition). The Scriptures are understood in the light of a particular tradition that is safeguarded by some sort of authoritative body. It can take the simple form of children's Sunday school materials at a Stone-Campbell Church of Christ that have the approbation of the congregation's elders. The materials, while geared *around* the Bible, offer *more* than the plain text of the Bible. They pass along the traditional understanding of Scripture that meets with the local authoritative body's approval.

There is nothing wrong with this. In fact, it is inescapable. The problem for Protestants, however, is that their traditions (the doctrinal understandings that form their interpretive framework) and magisterial structures all came into being more than a thousand years after Jesus established His Church. As a result, many of the beliefs that make up their distinctive traditions are at odds with the beliefs of the earliest Christians (as can be seen from the patristic citations in Appendix A). Furthermore, those who exercise magisterial authority stand outside the continuity of the apostolic Church and, therefore, are fundamentally *self-appointed,* or at least appointed by the larger body precisely because they already subscribe to the group's positions.

In a Stone-Campbell Church of Christ, for example, the local congregation will select men to be overseers (bishops). One of their functions is to safeguard the flock from false teachings. Teachings are judged to be false precisely because they contradict the already existing doctrinal norms, or traditions, of the congregation. These same norms also were utilized as litmus tests when the overseers were selected. The irony, however, is that the congregation has selected men to maintain the *status quo* of their tradition while believing that it is the truths of Scripture they are defending.

Our Lord promised that those who abide in His Word would *know* the Truth (John 8:1-32). They would not have to simply hope that they had the truth; they would *know* the truth. As a Church of Christ preacher, I tended to stop at that point and exclaim, "See! If we just read the Bible, we will know the truth!" When our Lord spoke these words, however, the Bible as such did not exist, so that could not have been His intended meaning.

Additionally, the sharp disagreements experienced between devout, Bible-reading Church of Christ members underscore the inadequacy of such an interpretation of Jesus' words. This is why our Lord also promised that He would send the Holy Spirit to guide the Apostles into *all* the Truth (John 14:25-26).

Evangelicals and Pentecostals often emphasize this promise of Christ and see it as the key to attaining certitude in understanding. The promise, however, was given primarily to the *Apostles* and not to individual believers. Additionally, Evangelicals and Pentecostals have not fared any better than Churches of Christ in this matter. While believing that the Holy Spirit guides them into all the truth, they cannot come to agreement on many essential matters.

The problem is that both of these approaches to the truth are missing an essential element: the *Church*. The Scriptures show that after the Holy Spirit descended at Pentecost, the Church—guided by the Apostles and their successors—became the "pillar and bulwark of the truth" (1 Timothy 3:15). When this is taken together with the two promises of our Lord previously mentioned, we see the essential relationship that truth has to the Word of God, the Holy Spirit, and the Church.

Christ and His Word are inseparable because Jesus Christ is the Incarnate Word of God (John 1:14). Christ and His Church are also inseparable, because the Church is His Body (Colossians 1:18). Therefore, because both the Word and the Church have no identity apart from Christ, the two have an essential relationship to one another. One cannot have the fullness of the Word of Christ without the fullness of the Body of Christ, the Church. This fullness of relationship with the Body of Christ results from full incorporation into the Church established by Jesus Christ and entrusted by Him with the full deposit of faith. Scripture and history both identify the Catholic Church as *that* Church.

This realization enables Catholics to live the Christian faith to its fullest. It does so by setting them free from the uncertainty that so often besets those attempting to operate in the *sola Scriptura* mode. Ironically, Protestants often consider themselves to be "free" and view Catholics as "shackled" to official Church dogma. It is precisely because the Catholic faith is unchanging and goes back to our Lord Jesus Christ Himself that Catholics are *truly* free. They are free to live the faith and plumb its depths instead of engaging in the never-ending struggle of reinventing the wheel by defining for themselves the content of the *true* faith.

I can remember the doctrinal struggles I faced as a Church of Christ preacher. Those struggles were rooted in the fact that good, reputable, and scholarly brethren often disagree over controversial issues of crucial consequence. Even more unsettling was the recognition of *personal* irresolution concerning these same issues. This irresolution did, at times, result in doctrinal vacillation. I do not believe, however, that I was unique in this regard. After all, how many preachers can honestly say that they have never changed their views on various controversial subjects? Yet, to recognize the reality of such positional shifts in the past is to undermine the certitude with which one can preach in the present, for the future may indeed bring to light a different understanding. This realization alone provides sufficient reason for any minister to pause before mounting the pulpit.

This, then, is what brings us to one of the most beautiful gifts that God has given us in the Catholic Church. This gift is the ability to embrace the fullness of the faith, confident that the Word of God, as the Church presents it, is the Word of Christ in its *fullness*. This confidence is not rooted in arrogance or in presumption, but in the promise of Christ to be with His Church always, even until the end of the age (Matthew 28:18-20). A confidence that arises from the realization that for two thousand years the Catholic Church, guided by the Holy Spirit, has presented the unchanging fullness of the Christian faith to every generation. A confidence that enables the Catholic to follow the lead of the Church as she experiences the fullness of the Word of Christ through the legitimate development of her understanding of the deposit of faith over time (which is addressed in Appendix G). A confidence that comes from knowing that in St. Peter and his successors, the popes, our Lord has blessed us with a visible point of reference to which we can go for solid and reliable teaching in an ever-changing world (see Appendix H for a brief study on Peter and the Papacy). And it is a confidence that is, ultimately, an expression of great *humility* on the part of the Church and the individual believer.

This chapter began by recounting a conversation I once had with a co-worker. When he expressed his disdain for the Catholic Church's claim that she had been entrusted with the fullness of Christian truth, he undoubtedly did not think that *humility* factored into the equation. Yet, it does, because the Church's claims are not rooted in human presumption but in divine provision. It is the God-Man, Jesus Christ, who promised to build His Church and to send the Holy Spirit to be her Guide. It is the Word of God that tells us that the Church is "the pillar and bulwark of the truth." To deny these truths would not be an expression of true humility, for as St. Teresa of Avila noted, "Humility is truth." It is in humility that the Church acknowledges these truths and, by the grace of God, goes forth into the world to fulfill her mission.

In the same way, individual Catholics are not being obnoxious or exhibiting hubris when they acknowledge the divine origin of the Church's deposit of faith and the infallible nature of her official explications of it. They are simply recognizing that which our Lord Jesus Christ has willed and ordained. In fact, it was as a Protestant that I found myself most subject to the temptations of pride and presumption. Claiming to have no need for the teaching authority of the Catholic Church, I had essentially set myself up as pope, all the while claiming that the papacy itself was a perverse presumption. Like most Protestants, I reserved for myself the right to pass final judgment on the veracity of the doctrines and practices of any communion with which I associated (giving concrete expression to that judgment by finding another communion when the old one no longer suited me). Because my doctrinal positions were based upon my private interpretation of

Scripture, I was often tempted to be condescending toward other Christians with whom I had serious doctrinal disagreements. This was due, in part, to the assumptions underlying the *sola Scriptura* approach to authority that I had adopted. After all, if the Scriptures were truly perspicuous to the honest reader, then it was a forgone conclusion that serious disagreements in essential areas were attributable to the supposed fact that those with whom I disagreed were ignorant, mentally deficient, or somewhat less than honest.

To keep peace among my fellow brethren, I would categorize our smaller disagreements as simply being over "nonessentials." Making such a distinction between "essentials" and "nonessentials," however, involves the exercise of magisterial authority. The reason that splits and divisions exist among Churches of Christ is precisely because they cannot agree on what is "essential." In reality, the problem was the approach to authority itself.

In becoming Catholic and confessing the infallible nature of the Church's teaching, I have not found occasion to boast in myself. In what would I boast? I can hardly boast for having "discovered" that which has been there all along. In truth, my entering into full communion with the Catholic Church constitutes an implicit acknowledgement of the fact that I am too small, too weak, and too limited to be my own pope. I am not qualified to teach the Church. Rather, in genuine humility, I confess my need to be taught *by* the Church. In essence, I am Catholic not because I have all of the answers but because I need answers—answers that come from my Holy Mother, the Church, giving to me *Christ in the fullness of His Word.*

Chapter 14

# Christ in the Fullness of His Sacraments

*And they brought to him a man who was deaf and had an impediment in his speech; and they besought him to lay his hand upon him. And taking him aside from the multitude privately, he put his fingers into his ears, and he spat and touched his tongue; and looking up to heaven, he sighed, and said to him, "Eph'phatha," that is, "Be opened." And his ears were opened, his tongue was released, and he spoke plainly (Mark 7:32-35).*

The prophets had foretold that the Messiah would bring healing. It should come as no surprise, then, that the Gospels provide us with numerous historical accounts of the healing hands of Jesus bringing wholeness of body and soul to those whom He touched. He placed His fingers in the deaf man's ears and opened them. Making a paste of clay and spittle, he applied it to the blind man's eyes and gave him sight (John 9:1-7). Clearly, Jesus simply could have spoken and thereby granted healing. He could, in fact, have forgone even the spoken word. He had only to *will* it. So why then does He not only speak the word but also provide physical touch and employ material means? To ponder that question is to discover *Christ in the fullness of His sacraments.*

Would any Christian ever dream of asking, "Was it Jesus who opened the blind man's eyes, or was it the clay and the washing?" The question itself sounds absurd, because it is understood by all that it was *Jesus* who *granted* the healing while the clay and the washing were simply *means* employed by Jesus to *impart* the healing.

Yet when it comes to the matter of salvation, many non-Catholic Christians seem to think that if Jesus is our Savior, then sacraments are inconsequential. They fail to recognize that Jesus and His sacraments are not at odds with each other. Our Lord and Savior Jesus Christ *chose* to institute sacraments that serve as the conduits of His saving grace.

Take, for example, the sacrament of Baptism. Evangelical Protestants generally believe that because it is the blood of Jesus that washes away our sins, baptism does not—even *cannot*—be involved in the process. In their way of thinking, it is an "either/or" proposition. It is *either* the Blood of Jesus that washes away our sins *or* it is Baptism that washes away our sins. The teaching of Scripture and the testimony of the early Church, however, show us that it is both (Scripture citations are provided in the footnotes of Chapter 3 and citations from the Early Church Fathers are in Appendix A). It *is* the blood of Jesus that washes away our sins *when* we are baptized. It is Christ who saves us *by means of* the graces He gives to us in the sacraments.

Part of the problem is that many non-Catholic Christians simply do not understand what is meant by the term "sacrament." For the sake of clarity, the Catechism of the Catholic Church provides the following definition: "Sacrament: An efficacious sign of grace, instituted by Christ and entrusted to the Church, by which divine life is dispensed to us through the work of the Holy Spirit."[14]

From this definition, please note the following about sacraments:

1. As *"efficacious signs of grace,"* the sacraments actually communicate, or convey, the graces that they signify. The washing that baptism signifies is actually

accomplished at that moment—*by grace* (cf. Acts 22:16, Ephesians 5:26, and Titus 3:5-7).

2.  The sacraments were instituted by Christ and entrusted to the Church. We see this with baptism when our Lord issued the Great Commission (Matthew 28:18-20).

3.  Through the sacraments, the Holy Spirit dispenses to us the very life of God or His "divine life" (*grace*). We see this most superlatively in the Sacrament of Holy Communion, whereby Christ imparts to us His life (see the citations provided in Appemdix A).

Thus it is not a matter of choosing between Jesus and His sacraments. They are *His* sacraments. *He* designed them. *He* instituted them. *He* has chosen to use them as the ordinary means of giving us grace. Moreover, *He* is the One who is ultimately ministering in each of them. As stated in the Catechism of the Catholic Church, "Celebrated worthily, the sacraments confer the grace they signify. They are *efficacious* because in them Christ Himself is at work: it is He who baptizes, He who acts in His sacraments in order to communicate the grace that each sacrament signifies."[15]

Should this surprise us? Not if we consider that it is *God* who created the material world and gave to us *both* a body and a soul. God likes matter. He made it and He declared it to be good (Genesis 1:31). What is more, God bestowed His ultimate blessing on the material universe when, by His Incarnation, the Second Person of the Most Holy Trinity assumed for Himself a human nature. Therefore, it should not seem strange to see our Lord, who redeems us body and soul, employ sacraments in applying to our souls the salvation He obtained for us on Calvary.

In coming to know Christ in the fullness of His sacraments, two of the seven sacraments have stood out in a special way. These were the ones that, as a Protestant, I found to be the most offensive. They are the Sacrament of Confession and the Most Blessed Sacrament of the Eucharist.

Regarding the Sacrament of Confession, also referred to as the Sacrament of Penance or Reconciliation, that which I had thought to be a perverse presumption has proven to be an avenue of divine grace. Every child who receives Christian instruction learns the story of the paralyzed man whose friends brought him before Jesus by lowering him through the roof of the house where Jesus was teaching (Mark 2:1-12). You may recall that Jesus, after looking at this helpless, pitiable man, said to him, "My son, your sins are forgiven." St. Mark tells us that these words of our Lord elicited indignation from the scribes who were present. They thought to themselves, "Why does this man speak thus? It is blasphemy! Who can forgive sins but God alone?" What was Jesus' response? He simply said, "Why do you question thus in your hearts? Which is easier, to say to the paralytic, 'Your sins are forgiven,' or to say, 'Rise, take up your pallet and walk'? *But that you may know that the Son of man has authority on earth to forgive sins...*I say to you, rise, take up your pallet and go home.'"

As a Protestant, I used to *long* to hear those same words from Jesus: *"My son, your sins are forgiven."* As a Church of Christ preacher, I delivered many sermons on the assurance of salvation. Invariably whenever I did, there would be people thanking me after the sermon, telling me how much it had helped them. The problem was that it never seemed to help *me!* Peace continued to elude me. The perennial presence of sin in my life caused me to continually question my own salvation.

We had a song in our Church of Christ hymnal entitled "Did You Fully Repent?" I would often reason to myself that, surely, if I had *fully* repented, I would not find myself so beset by habitual sins. I honestly cannot recall how many times I walked the aisle of a church seeking the spiritual strength I needed in order to live the faith I professed. More than once I thought that something was lacking at the time of my baptism. Consequently, I was baptized on three different occasions within the Church of Christ. Every time, without fail, the same old sins would quickly reappear and drive me to the point of despair. The resultant doubts and anxiety were at times more than I could bear. Once, for example, I had to be helped out of the church building because I had blacked out during the Lord's Supper due to the stress of trying to make certain that I was not partaking "in an unworthy manner" (cf. 1 Corinthians 11:27).

Other preachers tried to console me, every Scripture passage that taught the assurance of salvation for true believers seemed to be bracketed by other verses explaining that true believers were not folks who continued to sin. For example, I was often shown 1 John 5:13: "I write this to you who believe in the name of the Son of God, that you may know that you have eternal life." But earlier in the same epistle, we find: "By this we may be sure that we are in Him: he who says he abides in Him ought to walk in the same way in which He walked" (1 John 2:5-6). Even more distressing are the words found in the next chapter: "No one who abides in Him sins; no one who sins has either seen him or known Him" (1 John 3:6).

Yes, the same Epistle clarifies the matter somewhat by noting that it is possible for the believer to sin (1 John 2:1), even a sin unto death (1 John 5:16-17). The problem, however, was not so much the ability to accept the forgiveness of Christ after initial justification as it was determining whether initial justification had actually been received based upon the reality of subsequent moral failure. This left me in the agonizing position of trying to determine whether *my* faith was truly a saving faith.

I began to wish that I had been born in first-century Palestine along the pathway trod by Jesus. Maybe then, like the paralytic, I could have heard those soothing words from the lips of the Savior: *"My son, your sins are forgiven."* I began to lament that Jesus apparently left no sure way for individuals to hear those consoling words from Him. Such a privilege, it seemed, was for the relatively few souls blessed enough to have been in the right place at the right time.

My lamentation turned to expectation when I learned that Jesus had indeed made provision for me to hear His voice speak to the desperate needs of my own poor soul. That provision is found in St. John's Gospel: "Jesus said to them again, 'Peace be with you. As the Father has sent Me, even so I send you.' And when He had said this, He breathed on them, and said to them, 'Receive the Holy Spirit. If you forgive the sins of any, they are forgiven; if you retain the sins of any, they are retained'" (John 20:21-23).

These verses show us that Jesus sent out his Apostles and, by implication, their successors in the same way that the Father had sent Him. Through them, Jesus would continue to touch souls and change lives. Through the Church—*the Body of Christ*—Jesus would continue to walk among men in every generation. Through the ministers of the Church, He would continue to speak the words of absolution and bring forgiveness and peace to souls bedraggled by sin. In other words, in the Sacrament of Confession, people of every generation would be able to hear the voice of Jesus say, *"My son, your sins are forgiven. Arise, take up your mat and walk."*

It is for this reason that Catholic priests are said to act *in persona Christi Capitas* whenever they absolve sins. They are acting in the person of Jesus Christ. Hence, St. Paul told the Corinthians that he forgave sins "in the person of Christ" (2 Corinthians 2:10). While most modern English translations render this passage as "in the presence of Christ," the original Greek text uses the word *prosopon*. This word was used by the Council of Ephesus (A.D. 431) and the Council of Chalcedon

(A.D. 451) in their dogmatic pronouncements concerning the person of Jesus Christ. The significant point is that the bishops at these two councils spoke *koine* Greek, the original language of the New Testament, as their first language and wrote their documents in that language. They were not simply scholars translating a language that was not their native tongue. They were, rather, native speakers of the same language in which St. Paul wrote to the Corinthians, and they used the word *prosopon* in reference to a person.

Looking back, I can remember pitying Catholics for *having* to go to Confession. Now, having received innumerable graces from Jesus through this great sacrament, my heart goes out to my separated Protestant brethren who are unable to experience the healing hand of Jesus in this priceless treasure that He has entrusted to His Church.

Regarding the Most Blessed Sacrament of the Eucharist, that which I formerly regarded as an unspeakable blasphemy I have now come to see as *"the source and summit of the Christian life."** Eucharist is the most common Catholic designation used for what Protestants typically refer to as "the Lord's Supper." It is rooted in the terminology employed by our Lord in the Upper Room when He instituted Holy Communion. In Matthew 26:27, it states that after "he had given thanks," our Lord gave His disciples the Cup of His Blood. The words, "he had given thanks," are from the Greek *eucharisteo*, from which we get the word "Eucharist."

As a Church of Christ member, I faithfully participated in the weekly observance of the Lord's Supper. It was *not* the Eucharist, however. Like most Protestants, I believed that the Lord's Supper was strictly symbolic. The unleavened bread and

---

* As stated in the *Catechism of the Catholic Church* (No. 1324), "The Eucharist is 'the source and summit of the Christian life.' 'The other sacraments, and indeed all ecclesiastical ministries and works of the apostolate, are bound up with the Eucharist and are oriented toward it.'"

*"fruit of the vine"* were exactly that, nothing more and nothing less. The Lord's Supper was not considered a sacrament in the sense that grace, *per se*, was somehow conferred by this weekly observance. It was a memorial that could impact one's life only to the extent of one's ability to conceptualize and internalize the meaning of the observance. The Eucharist, however, is different.

Two thousand years ago, on the shores of the Sea of Galilee, our Lord Jesus Christ made a most astounding announcement. Having miraculously fed more than 5,000 souls with a mere five loaves and two fish, He proceeded to announce that He is the Bread of Life (John 6:35). Moreover, He proclaimed that the Bread to which He was referring was His very own sacred *Body* (John 6:51). But He didn't stop there. He went on to say that the only way to have His life in us is to eat His Body and drink His Blood (John 6:53-56).

For 2,000 years, Catholic Christians have understood these mysterious words of our Blessed Lord in the context of the Eucharist. It is in the celebration of the Eucharist that the Sacred Body and the Precious Blood of our Lord and Savior Jesus Christ are made present to us under the *appearance* of bread and wine. It is in receiving Holy Communion that we come to share more fully in His divine life. In fact, the reason Catholics refer to the Sacrament of the Eucharist as *"the Most Blessed Sacrament"* is because in this sacrament we not only receive the *grace* of God but *God Himself*. As stated in the Catechism, "For in the blessed Eucharist is contained the whole spiritual good of the Church, namely Christ himself, our Pasch."[16] The Second Person of the Most Holy Trinity is made substantially present to us in this greatest of sacraments. And yet, it is precisely this Sacrament that most often falls under attack.

Most non-Catholics maintain that our Lord's words in John 6:35-71 offer no foundation for the Catholic belief in the Real Presence of Christ in the Eucharist. They believe that our Lord's words were merely metaphorical and meant simply to convey the concept of consuming Christ in a figurative way—to see Him as our source of spiritual life and nourishment. Protestant Christians often point out that St. John records several metaphors employed by Christ in describing Himself. For example, did not Jesus say, "I am the true vine" (John 15:1) and "I am the door of the sheep" (John 10:7). Yet, whereas the words used by Jesus to liken Himself to a door are specifically said, in John 10:6, to constitute a *figure of speech*, nothing of the sort is ever said in the "bread of Life" discourse of John 6. The details of the John 6 discourse cast Jesus' claim to be "the bread of life" in a somewhat different mold than the other "I am" statements recorded in John's Gospel. The specific words of Jesus, and the reaction of those who heard Him, simply do not admit a merely metaphorical interpretation. Please consider the following points from the text:

1.  Jesus gave no indication whatsoever that He was speaking figuratively.

In fact, He moved from a very generalized concept of being "the bread which came down out of heaven" in John 6:41, a description that could be understood metaphorically, to a specific definition of the "bread" that He would offer—and that we must eat—as His "flesh" (John 6:51, 53-56). In other words, if Jesus had simply stated, "I am the bread that came down out of heaven" and had left it at that, it would be reasonable to assume that He was simply employing a figure of speech. But he did not leave it at that. He elaborated considerably and very specifically, something He did not do in any of the other "I am" statements. He definitively identified the bread of which He spoke as His own flesh. Moreover, as if to remove any doubt in regard to what He meant by "flesh," He stated specifically that He was referring to the flesh that He would *"offer for the life of the world."* In other words, the

Sacred Body offered by Christ on Calvary's cross is what we must eat if we are to have life.

2.  There is no metaphorical parallel between "bread" and "flesh" in either the Scriptures or in common parlance.

In other words, when we consider the other "I am" statements made by Jesus, we see a metaphorical parallel between the figure employed by Christ and the truth He is seeking to convey. When opening the blind man's eyes to the natural light of day, for example, Jesus proclaims, "I am the light of the world" (John 9:5). When speaking of the necessity of abiding in Him in order to bear lasting fruit, Jesus likens Himself to a vine upon which we are branches (John 15:5). When speaking of the need to be wary of false shepherds, He declares Himself to be the "door of the sheep" and the "Good Shepherd" (John 10:1-14). In each of these instances, the parallel concepts are all obvious and apparent. When we come to John 6, however, things change. There is no obvious metaphorical parallel between Jesus being the *"bread from Heaven"* and our need to *"eat* (His) *flesh and drink* (His) *blood."*

The words of J. Pohle, from his article in the *Catholic Encyclopedia* entitled "The Real Presence of Christ in the Eucharist" are especially insightful on this point.

> The necessity of the natural sense is not based upon the absurd assumption that Christ could not in general have resorted to the use of figures, but upon the evident requirement of the case, which demand that He did not, in a matter of such paramount importance, have recourse to meaningless and deceptive metaphors. For figures enhance the clearness of speech only when the figurative meaning is obvious, either from the nature of the case (*e.g.* from a reference to a statue of Lincoln, by saying: 'This is Lincoln') or from the usages of common parlance (*e.g.*

in the case of this synecdoche: 'This glass is wine'). Now, neither from the nature of the case nor in common parlance is bread an apt or possible symbol of the human body. Were one to say of a piece of bread, 'This is Napoleon,' he would not be using a figure, but uttering nonsense. There is but one means of rendering a symbol improperly so called clear and intelligible, namely, by conventionally settling beforehand what it is to signify, as, for instance, if one were to say: 'Let us imagine these two pieces of bread before us to be Socrates and Plato.' Christ, however, instead of informing His Apostles that he intended to use such a figure, told them rather the contrary in the discourse containing the promise: 'the bread that I will give is my flesh, for the life of the world' (John 6:52). Such language, of course, could be used only by a God-man; so that belief in the Real Presence necessarily presupposes belief in the true Divinity of Christ.[17]

3.  His original audience understood Him to be speaking literally, not figuratively (John 6:52, 60).

As a direct result of His words, the Scriptures tell us that "many of His disciples drew back and no longer went about with Him" (John 6:66). Notice here that it was His disciples who no longer walked with Him, not His enemies or merely curious bystanders. If they had simply misunderstood Jesus by interpreting Jesus' words literally when He actually intended them to be understood figuratively, we have the rather incredible prospect of Jesus allowing His followers to stumble over a simple and easily clarified misunderstanding. Yet Jesus made no attempt to correct the alleged misunderstanding. Instead, He turned to the Twelve and said, "Will you also go away?" (John 6:67). In so doing, our Lord confirmed that He was willing to let them leave as well if they did not receive this teaching. It should be noted that Protestants often claim that Jesus' words in John 6:63 clarify the issue and indicate that He was speaking figuratively. He said,

> It is the spirit that gives life, the flesh is of no avail; the words that I have spoken to you are spirit and life.

First, note that *nowhere* in Scripture or in the contemporary manner of speaking are the words "spirit" and "figurative" even remotely construed as synonyms. To assert that such is the case here is to do violence to both the Word of God and to language in general.

Furthermore, such an interpretation of these words would have Jesus talking out of both sides of His mouth. No less than three times in the preceding verses, Jesus said we *must* eat His flesh and drink His blood. Are we to believe that He is now saying that to do so would be fruitless because *"the flesh profits nothing?"* Obviously Jesus was not telling His hearers that it is pointless to do the very thing that He had just taught them they *must* do. So what *was* He saying? He was simply emphasizing that He was talking about a deep spiritual truth, not the mere feeding of their physical bodies, which had been the actual reason most of His audience had followed Him (cf. John 6:26-27). He was not recommending that they pluck off bits of His flesh for their physical sustenance, for that would be cannibalism. Rather, Jesus was revealing the truth that His flesh—*supernaturally supplied* through the Eucharist—will impart to their souls His very life by the power of the Holy Spirit.

That Jesus' Bread of Life discourse in John 6 is a prelude to the Eucharist is made clear by the fact that Scripture does not record Him speaking in such terms again until He institutes the Eucharist in the Upper Room the night before His passion and death. It is there that He takes bread and says, *"This is My Body."* It is there that He takes wine and says, *"This is My Blood"* (Matthew 26:26-28). Every major Protestant version of the Scriptures renders these words of our Lord the same way: "This *is* My Body...this *is* My Blood." None of them translates the original Greek, *estin*, as *"represents"* or *"signifies."* This is important to note because many Protestant commentators and apologists will assert that the original Greek *can* be translated, *"This represents My Body...this signifies My Blood."* Yet the Protestant linguists and scholars who have put together the major Protestant translations of the Scriptures say otherwise. They all, without exception, stick to the literal translation of the Greek and render our Lord's words the same way that the Catholic Church has for 2,000 years.

Moreover, there is nothing in the text to indicate that Jesus was speaking metaphorically. Once again, J. Pohle aptly notes,

> In all the languages of the world the expression 'my body' designates a person's natural body, not the mere sign or symbol of that body. True it is that the Scriptural words 'Body of Christ' not infrequently have the meaning of 'Church', which is called the mystical Body of Christ, a figure easily and always discernible as such from the text or context (cf. Colossians 1:24). This mystical sense, however, is impossible in the words of Institution, for the simple reason that Christ did not give the Apostles His Church to eat, but His Body, and that 'body and blood,' by reason of their real and logical association, cannot be separated from one another, and hence are all the less susceptible of a figurative use.[18]

The literal nature of His declaration is underscored by the very setting in which He made it—the celebration of the Jewish Passover. Recall that in the Passover, the sacrificial lamb *had to be eaten* by the faithful, or else they were cut off from the people. St. Paul tells us that Jesus Christ *is* our Passover (1 Corinthians 5:7). Accordingly, just like the Israelites observing the Passover, *we have to eat the Lamb*. The typology between the Passover and the Eucharist is truly striking. If the Israelites had to eat the Passover lamb, how then is that typology fulfilled if not by the Eucharist, especially since Jesus said we must eat His flesh and then subsequently announced that the bread of the Passover is His flesh? Are we to believe that Jesus fulfilled the symbolism of the Passover in a merely symbolic way? This does not make sense in light of the fact that in all Old Testament typology, the New Testament fulfillment is always more glorious than that which foreshadowed it. This typology, however, is not fulfilled if Jesus spoke only metaphorically.

As we continue through the New Testament Scriptures, we see that St. Paul understood our Lord's words literally and not figuratively. He rhetorically asked the Corinthian Christians, "The cup of blessing which we bless, is it not a participation (or, "communion," *KJV*) in the Blood of Christ? The bread which we break, is it not a participation in the Body of Christ?" (1 Corinthians 10:16) He went on to tell them, "Whoever, therefore, eats the bread or drinks the cup of the Lord in an unworthy manner will be guilty of profaning the Body and Blood of the Lord" (1 Corinthians 11:27). Protestant apologists often claim that these words of St. Paul disprove the Catholic belief in the Real Presence of Christ in the Eucharist. After all, does not St. Paul speak of "the *bread* which we break"? In so doing is he not indicating that the bread remains simply that—bread? The short answer is "No."

The consecrated bread and wine which have become the Sacred Body and Precious Blood of Christ can still be properly referred to as "Bread" and "Wine" without in any way denying or diminishing the actual, substantial change that has taken place. Such, in fact, was the understanding of the early Christians. Consider the following words from St. Justin Martyr:

> For not as common bread nor common drink do we receive these; but since Jesus Christ our Savior was made incarnate by the word of God and had both flesh and blood for our salvation, so too, as we have been taught, the food which has been made into the Eucharist by the Eucharistic prayer set down by him, and by the change of which our blood and flesh is nurtured, is both the flesh and the blood of that incarnated Jesus.[19]

In other words, he referred to the Eucharistic elements as "bread" and "drink" while making it clear that they were not *ordinary* bread and wine. They were, in fact, the Body and Blood of Jesus Christ.

It remains to consider in what sense, or senses, the Eucharistic Body and Blood of Christ may be properly referred to as "bread" and "wine." There are at least three senses in which this may be done: *manner*, *effect*, and *appearance*. In regard to *manner*, the Eucharistic Body and Blood of Christ are consumed in the same manner as are bread and wine. In regard to *effect*, the Eucharistic Body and Blood of Christ nourish and inebriate the soul as do bread and wine the body. In regard to *appearance*, the Eucharistic Body and Blood of Christ retain the accidents, or outward appearances, of bread and wine.

It is this last sense—that of *appearance*—that is most often derided by those who deny the Catholic belief in the Real Presence of Christ in the Eucharist. Appealing to what seems logical, they claim that if it looks like bread, feels like bread, and tastes like bread, then it must *be* bread. As reasonable as that approach may be in the purely *natural* order, it fails to take into account the proper distinction between *substance* and *accidents* while, at the same time, overlooking the realities of the *supernatural* order.

Simply put, *substance* refers to the foundation or principle that makes something what it is, whereas *accidents* are those properties that can be perceived by the senses. In the natural order, we have come to expect certain accidents to be associated with certain substances. For example, the substance we call water has certain perceptible accidents, depending upon environmental conditions. Whereas water has a solid appearance at its freezing point, it becomes a colorless, tasteless liquid at room temperature, and then a cloudy vapor at its boiling point. It is precisely these accidents, or properties, that enable us to distinguish water from other substances.

In the supernatural order, however, the rigid correlation of certain substances with a particular set of accidents can be suspended. The Sacred Scriptures reveal to us instances when such has occurred. Fluid water does not normally provide a suitable surface on which men can walk. However, both Jesus and St. Peter walked on water.

Even more telling are the numerous instances of angelic appearances to men. Take the appearance of the "three men" to Abraham by the oaks of Mamre (Genesis 18:1-2). Two of these "men" are specifically said to be "angels" (Genesis 19:1). The Bible, however, defines angels as "ministering spirits" (Hebrews 1:13-14), and spirits, by definition, are immaterial beings, meaning they do not have physical bodies. Yet these angels took on physical form and ate with Abraham (Genesis 18:8). They looked so much like men, in fact, that the depraved inhabitants of Sodom attempted to rape them (Genesis 19:4-5). They looked like men, ate like men, spoke like men, yet they were *not* men. They were angels who *supernaturally* appeared as men. In the supernatural order, things are not always what they appear to be. Nowhere is this truth more profoundly expressed than in the Eucharist, where what appears to be only bread is, by the mysterious grace of God, the adorable and life-giving Sacred Body of Jesus Christ. It is a supernatural reality, the belief in which is rooted firmly in the words of the God-Man, Jesus Christ, who declared it to be so.

The Scriptures themselves seem to be plain enough on the subject. For the sake of discussion, however, let us admit the possibility for a divergence in plausible interpretations. It is then that we can turn to the Fathers of the Church, the earliest post-apostolic Christians on record. Their writings reveal how the first, second, and third generations of believers understood the words of Jesus and the teachings of His Apostles.

It needs to be mentioned that when referring to the Fathers of the Church, Catholics do not pit the Fathers against the Scriptures, as some might suggest. Rather, Catholics go to the writings of the early Fathers in order to show how the first Christians understood the Scriptures. Keep in mind that these are the Christians who were taught by the Apostles themselves or their immediate successors. Keep in mind, also, that these are the Christians who became the early martyrs whom all Christians venerate. Doesn't it make sense that we should at least consider how *they* understood the words of Scripture?

Among these early writers are St. Ignatius of Antioch (A.D. 110) and St. Justin Martyr (A.D. 150), both of whom were martyrs for the faith. St. Ignatius was the bishop of Antioch and wrote his now-famous letters while on his way to be martyred in Rome. They were, in essence, his parting words to the Church. In his letter to the Christians in Ephesus (A.D. 110), he wrote:

> "Give ear to the bishop and to the presbytery with an undivided mind, breaking one Bread, which is the medicine of immortality, the antidote against death, enabling us to live forever in Jesus Christ."[20]

Writing to the Church at Smyrna, this same martyred bishop said:

> "Take note of those who hold heterodox opinions...they abstain from the Eucharist and from prayer, because they do not confess that the Eucharist is the Flesh of our Savior Jesus Christ, Flesh which suffered for our sins and which the Father, in His goodness, raised up again."[21]

In the passage cited earlier, St. Justin Martyr testifies to the faith of the early Church by explicitly stating that the "bread" and "drink" of the Eucharist are "the flesh and the blood of that incarnated Jesus."[22]

So strong was the early Church's conviction concerning the Real Presence of Christ in the Eucharist that it did not undergo a serious challenge until the time of Berengarious of Tours in the eleventh century. In other words, for the first thousand years of the Church's existence, Christians universally believed that the bread and wine of the Eucharist were the actual Body and Blood of Jesus Christ made sacramentally available to them as the manna they would need to journey through the wilderness of this life and enter into the eternal rest of the Promised Land.

The preceding citations from both Sacred Scripture and the Church Fathers conclusively demonstrate that the Catholic belief in the Real Presence of Christ in the Eucharist is *not* some "medieval invention," as is often asserted by anti-Catholic polemicists. Rather, it is a core element of the very deposit of faith entrusted by Christ to the Apostles and for which the early Christian martyrs gave their lives.

Christians who deny this truth, or who, through no fault of their own, are ignorant of this truth, are missing a great gift. One of the greatest tragedies of the sixteenth century Protestant Reformation was the loss of apostolic succession on the part of the resulting Protestant denominations. In rejecting the Catholic faith, the Protestant Reformers abandoned the sacrament of Holy Orders whereby men are ordained to the priestly ministry and given the ability by Christ to confect the Eucharist. This Sacrament of Holy Orders was instituted by Christ at the same time He also instituted the Eucharist in the Upper Room. In saying to his Apostles, *"Do this"* (Luke 22:19), Jesus not only gave them a command, he gave them the *ability* to carry out that command—namely, to do for others what he was doing for them in giving them his Body and Blood. That ability would be transmitted by the Apostles to their successors—the bishops— and to other men whom they would ordain to the ministry. This is why we find St. Ignatius of Antioch writing, "Let that be considered a valid Eucharist which is celebrated by the bishop, or by one whom he appoints. Wherever the bishop appears, let the people be there; just as wherever Jesus Christ is, there is the Catholic Church."[23]

As a result, Protestant ministers are able to offer their flocks *only* bread and wine but *not* the actual Sacred Body and Precious Blood of our Lord Jesus Christ under the appearance of bread and wine in the Most Blessed Sacrament of the Eucharist. Correspondingly, Catholics who take a nonchalant posture toward the Eucharist risk incurring judgment upon their souls.

The gift of the Blessed Sacrament is one way in which our blessed Lord fulfilled His promise to be with His Church always. It could be rightly said that He never left the earth, for He remains here, among us, in the Blessed Sacrament.

We began this chapter with the account of Jesus opening the deaf man's ears. The first words this poor man heard must have been the most beautiful words he had ever heard, for they were the words of Jesus. The most beautiful words to ever fall on my ears have been those of our Lord in the context of His sacraments: the Sacrament of Holy Matrimony, when Gloria said, "I do;" the Sacrament of Reconciliation, when Jesus, through the agency of His priests, pronounced the words of absolution; and my first Holy Communion, when Father Bill Casey said, "The Body of Christ." In and through the sacraments, I have truly been given *Christ in His Fullness*.

Chapter 15

# Christ in the Fullness of Worship

*The woman said to Him, 'Sir, I perceive that You are a prophet. Our fathers worshiped on this mountain; and You say that in Jerusalem is the place where men ought to worship.' Jesus said to her, 'Woman, believe Me, the hour is coming when neither on this mountain nor in Jerusalem will you worship the Father. You worship what you do not know; we worship what we know, for salvation is from the Jews. But the hour is coming, and now is, when the true worshipers will worship the Father in spirit and truth, for such the Father seeks to worship Him. God is spirit, and those who worship Him must worship in spirit and truth' (John 4:19-24).*

As a Church of Christ member, I was well acquainted with this passage from St. John's Gospel. The Stone-Campbell Churches of Christ place great emphasis on the need to worship God *"in spirit and truth."* Church of Christ members tend to interpret this to mean worshiping with the proper attitude (or "spirit") and according to divinely revealed norms (or "truth"). It would not be unfair for me to state that, in my experience, the "spirit" aspect of worship was for the most part largely assumed, whereas a great deal of stress was placed upon the outward particulars of worship. In fact, the Stone-Campbell Movement experienced one of its primary internal divisions over one of the outward particulars of worship, namely whether it is acceptable to use musical instruments in worship. The Churches of Christ, with whom Gloria and I were associated, believed that the New Testament Scriptures did not authorize mechanical instruments for use in worship. Our congregational singing was strictly *a capella* (without instrumental accompaniment). This background fostered in me an approach to worship that was concerned primarily with doing things "right."*

Did I try to offer the Lord heartfelt worship? Yes. However, my primary motivation for attending Sunday services was the sense of obligation and the fear of incurring the debt of sin if I did not. That is not to say that I never enjoyed worship services or benefited from them. But as a believing Catholic, my experience of worship has been completely different. While I am indeed obligated to attend Sunday Mass and commit a sin if I fail to do so without a serious reason, this obligation is not burdensome. It is a deep and profound *privilege*. This difference in perspective is not attributable to the music, the preaching, the décor, or the fellowship. It is due to the fact that Christ is substantially and truly present—*body, blood, soul, and divinity*—in the Most Blessed Sacrament of the Eucharist. His Real Presence is the difference.

While it is true that Christ is present wherever two or more are gathered in His name (Matthew 18:20), it could be said that all people—even unbelievers—are ever and always in God's presence (cf. Psalm 139:7-10). We are talking about a *kind* of presence. For example, to simply exist is to be in the presence of God in one sense, whereas to gather together with other Christians is to be in His presence in another sense. To hear the Word of God as it is proclaimed from the Scriptures is to be in God's presence in yet another sense. To have been before the incarnate Christ

---

* This is not to say that giving attention to the particulars of worship is a bad thing. The Catholic Church, for example, has carefully defined liturgical norms that govern the particulars of public worship. These are good and necessary. However, they are not an end in themselves.

as He walked the shores of the Sea of Galilee was an even more profound and tangible way of being in God's presence. Now, after Christ's ascension back into heaven, the most profound and tangible avenue of being in God's presence that is available to all is to adore Him in the Most Blessed Sacrament, present in Catholic churches around the world.

Ironically, before becoming a Catholic Christian, I was under the impression that liturgical worship and ritual were by nature cold, stale, and dead. As a Church of Christ member, I had been taught that there existed a sharp dichotomy between the worship of the Old Testament and the worship of the New Testament. I was told that the worship of the Old Covenant was "physical," whereas the worship of the New Covenant was "spiritual." This perspective was given concrete expression when one of my instructors, in addressing the question of musical instruments in worship, said, "Music under the old Law was played on the *harp*; music in the Church is to be played on the *heart*." As a result, ritual and liturgy were considered throwbacks to Judaism and, therefore, out of place in Christian worship. The elaborate liturgy of the Catholic Church was thought to be out of harmony with the "simple" worship of the early Church and, as a result, offensive to God.

History, however, reveals to us that the "simple" worship of the early Church was unmistakably similar to the modern Catholic Mass. For example, consider the following excerpts from the liturgy as witnessed by St. Hippolytus of Rome who wrote around the year A.D. 215:

> And when he has been made bishop let all salute him with the kiss of peace, because of his having been made worthy. The deacons shall then bring the offering to him; and he imposing his hand on it, along with all the presbytery, shall give thanks, saying: "The Lord be with you."

And all shall respond, "And with your spirit."
"Hearts aloft!"
"We keep them with the Lord."
"Let us give thanks to the Lord."
"It is right and just."

And then he shall continue immediately: "We give you thanks, O God, through your beloved Son Jesus Christ, whom in these last days you have sent as Savior and Redeemer and as the angel of Your will; He that is Your inseparable Word, through whom You made all things, and who is well-pleasing to You; whom you sent from heaven into the womb of a Virgin, and who, dwelling within her, was made flesh and was manifested as your Son, born of the Holy Spirit and of the Virgin; who, fulfilling Your will and winning for Himself a holy people, extended His hands when it was time for Him to suffer, so that by His suffering He might set free those who believed in You; who also, when He was betrayed to His voluntary suffering, in order that He might destroy death and break the bonds of the devil and trample hell underfoot and enlighten the just and set a boundary and show forth His resurrection, took bread and gave thanks to You, saying: 'Take, eat: this is My Body, which is broken for you.' Likewise with the Cup too, saying, 'This is My Blood with is poured out for you. Whenever you do this, you do it in My memory.'

"Remembering, therefore, His death and resurrection, we offer to You the bread and the cup, giving thanks to You, because of Your having accounted us worthy to stand before You and minister to You. And we pray that you might send Your Holy Spirit upon the offering of the holy Church. Gather as one in the fullness of the Holy Spirit Your saints who participate; and confirm their faith in truth so that we may praise and glorify You through Your Son Jesus Christ, through whom be glory and honor to You, to the Father and the Son with the Holy Spirit, in You holy Church, both now and through the ages of ages. Amen."[22]

The order and wording of these liturgical prayers, for all practical purposes, mirror the Eucharistic Prayers of the present-day Mass (specifically Eucharistic Prayer II, which is reproduced in Appendix C). When St. Hippolytus penned these words, he was bearing testimony to the liturgy as it was *already* being conducted in his day (c. A.D. 215). In other words, these prayers predate the time of St. Hippolytus, placing them at least back into the second century. The point is that the worship of the early Church was not quite as simple and undeveloped as some would like to believe. The Catholic Mass is not some mutation that developed over many centuries. The earliest writings available bear witness to a form of liturgical worship that is in complete harmony with the Mass.

This should not surprise us. After all, the Old Testament outlines a very developed form of liturgical worship for God's people under the Old Covenant, while the Book of Revelation depicts heaven as a place of endless liturgical worship. Therein we find lampstands (Rev. 1:12), liturgical chant (Rev. 4:8), an altar (Rev. 6:9), a heavenly temple (Rev. 7:15), and incense and censers (Rev. 8:3). If St. John were writing to a Church that no longer identified with such imagery, because it allegedly had become outmoded with the formation of the New Covenant, why would he employ such? Therefore, it is no surprise that we find, in the ages between these two, the New Testament Church on earth adoring God in sacred liturgy.

Some may object that the New Testament writings do not provide any of the liturgical details. I would counter, however, with, "That's exactly right." The New Testament writings do not go into a great deal of detail pertaining to the "mechanics" of worship. Rather, as is so often the case, they presume upon a body of common knowledge and practice (Tradition) that we subsequently find elaborated in greater detail in the writings of the early Church.

In reality, *all* corporate Christian worship involves *some* form of ritual and liturgy. There will be songs sung, prayers offered, and sermons delivered. Depending on the traditions of a particular denomination, there will be a certain frequency in observing the Lord's Supper, whereby our Lord's saving work is commemorated with *physical* bread and the *material* "fruit of the vine." Even the prayers that are ostensibly extemporaneous will give evidence to a certain form by addressing the same concerns with a recurring phraseology. Even those non-Catholic Christians who criticize the rituals and forms of Catholic worship are themselves ritualistic and liturgical to varying degrees.

Is there anything wrong with this? No. In fact, it is unavoidable. Moreover, not only is it unavoidable but it is *good.* It is through religious ritual that we remove ourselves from the humdrum of everyday life and enter into sacred space. We are, in effect, transported from the mundane to the ethereal.* While it is true that we can momentarily pause and offer God worship at any moment of any day, this does not mean that God does not call us to set aside specific times and occasions on which to offer Him specific acts of worship that He has prescribed. In addition, rather than dragging us into a "worship rut," the Mass opens the door to fully engaged adoration. The prayers of the liturgy allow us to truly *contemplate* the mysteries of which they speak, liberating us from the ensnaring and never-ending pursuit of novelty, a pursuit which effectively sidetracks us from true contemplation and adoration.

---

* For a fuller treatment of this, I strongly recommend *Evangelical is Not Enough* by Thomas Howard (San Francisco: Ignatius Press, 1988).

I can remember being troubled as a youth by the thought that heaven might be boring. Much of that was due, of course, to an understandable apprehension regarding the unknown. Yet when we look at the closing book of the Bible and see that heaven is depicted in terms of divine liturgy, it no longer is an unknown. We discover that the sacred liturgy, properly conducted on this earth, becomes a portal to heaven. With that in mind, I can remember when, shortly after being received into the Church, I was caught up in a particularly reverent Mass at the Fathers of Mercy and said to myself, "If heaven is like this, I'm all for it." I really could have continued doing what I was doing for all eternity, and it would not have been boring. I was experiencing *Christ in the fullness of worship.*

# Chapter 16

# *Christ in the Fullness of His Family*

Little Flower Catholic Church of Hollywood, Florida, was named in honor of St. Therese of the Child Jesus and the Holy Face. St. Therese was a nineteenth century Carmelite nun from Lisieux, France, and is known affectionately as the "Little Flower of Jesus" because in her childlike spirit she saw herself as a little flower in her beloved Lord's garden. Before passing from this life at the early age of twenty-four, she promised to send a shower of roses from heaven. The steeple of Little Flower Church was visible from my boyhood home. It was the first Catholic church that I ever entered. I attended Boy Scout meetings in her school building; I passed her each day on my way to high school; I can even remember thinking how embarrassing it would be to attend a school with a name like "Little Flower."

In the spring of 2005, God sent to Gloria and me the gift of our fifth child, whom we named Therese Marie Sullivan, in honor of the Little Flower of Jesus by whose intercessory prayers we had received so fragrant a rose.

One aspect of Catholic Christianity that often proves puzzling to Protestants is the way in which Catholics view their relationship with the saints in heaven. Both as a fundamentalist youth and as a Church of Christ preacher, I believed that the "dearly departed" were exactly that—*departed*. While we might erect memorials in their honor and think of them on occasion, we could not be said to have any true *relationship* with them this side of heaven. I had even heard it said that since the saints in heaven were in the presence of Jesus, they no longer had any thoughts for the likes of us still on earth. Nothing could be further from the beliefs of the early Christians and the teaching of the Catholic Church.

In the catacombs of Rome, inscriptions on early Christian tombs call upon saints in heaven to pray for the dearly departed. This is just one example of how the early Christians believed, as the Catholic Church still teaches today, that the saints in heaven and the saints on earth are members of one Body, the Church. Christ does not have two bodies made up of those who are on earth and another of those who have passed from this life to the next. He has only one Body and, together, they form a *family*. Like all truly functional families, the family of God is composed of members who are mindful of each other.

As a Church of Christ member, I had a rather truncated view of the family of God. For all practical purposes, it was narrowly defined to encompass only those believers who were members of the Stone-Campbell Churches of Christ. At that time, if I had been asked to compose a catalog of the greatest Christian saints throughout the centuries, I would have presented a canon that most Protestants and Catholics would find quite startling. It would have consisted almost exclusively of a number of venerable Church of Christ preachers from the nineteenth and twentieth centuries along with the usual Old and New Testament saints. The sixteenth century Protestant Reformers would have received "honorable mention," but then only with careful qualification. I considered them to be great men because of their opposition to the Roman Catholic Church, but nonetheless lacking because of their failure to grasp the "New Testament Pattern" as understood by the followers of Stone and

Campbell three centuries later. The early Church Fathers, of whom I was essentially ignorant, would not have made the list. My roll call of saints, therefore, would have been heavy on both ends with a gigantic 1,400 year gap in the middle.

To many, this will undoubtedly seem strange, even bizarre. But this is not all that unique. In fact, it is quite commonplace, with different denominations differing only in the particulars. Most Protestant denominations that have a "remnant mentality"— those who consider themselves the exclusive and relatively small "remnant" of the Lord's *truly* faithful people—identify themselves with the saints of Sacred Scripture. They believe that the Apostle Paul, for example, was a believer cut from the same bolt of cloth as they. The early Church Fathers along with the Church of the Middle Ages are viewed with deep suspicion, as are other Protestants whom they consider to be tainted, to varying degrees, with "Romanism." The "remnant" churches also construct canons of saints, heavy on both ends with the saints of the Bible on one end and their own group's founders and themselves on the other, with huge gaps in the middle.

Some are not troubled by these gaps, dismissing them as irrelevant. They believe that the Church simply experienced a massive apostasy, or falling away, and was not fully restored until the arrival of their particular movement. This view, however, does not square with Scripture (as was demonstrated in Chapter 10).

For others, however, these enormous gaps produce a measure of discomfort and concern. They know, almost intuitively, that the Lord's Church should have a continuous and dynamic presence on this earth. They find it disconcerting to believe that the family of God disappeared from view for more than a millennium. They tend to do either one of two things: (1) they assert that believers such as themselves have always existed *somewhere* in the nooks and crannies of the world but were overlooked by history, or (2) they assume that the various heretical sects that have cropped up throughout history were their own kindred spirits professing beliefs identical with their own.

The first option cannot be reconciled with Scripture (cf. Chapter 10) because the Lord did not intend His Church to be a clandestine, obscure institution unnoticed by the world. The second option cannot be reconciled with history, because the beliefs of both the early Church Fathers and the early heretical sects simply do not match those of modern Protestant denominations. Any solidarity between them and modern Protestant communions is contrived and imaginary.

As a Church of Christ preacher, I spent little time mulling over this problem. I avoided it and assumed that someday the pieces would all fall into place. Well, they eventually did, but not in the way I expected.

It was while reading the *Martyrdom of St. Polycarp* and the works of St. Ignatius of Antioch, St. Justin Martyr, and St. Irenaeus of Lyons that I came face-to-face with the reality that the teachings of the Roman Catholic Church reflect the beliefs of the most ancient Christian writers on record (see Appendix A for excerpts from these ancient writers). While this realization was troubling to me, in some respects it also brought with it a rather unexpected, almost subconscious, sigh of relief. This was rooted in the awareness that if the beliefs of the Catholic Church could, in fact, be traced back through all the centuries of the Christian era, back even to Apostolic times, then there were no gaps in the life of the Church. Christ had established His Church, and the gates of hell have not prevailed against it (Matthew 16:18ff). It was there all along, but my prejudices and preconceived ideas had obscured it from my sight. The family of God had proven to be far more extensive than I had previously imagined.

My subsequent readings of early Christian writings were, of course, still investigative in nature. I sought to ascertain what the earliest Christians on record actually believed on various topics, but my readings also took on an exhilarating air of discovery as I was introduced to a veritable myriad of brethren previously unknown to me. I was beginning to experience *Christ in the fullness of His family.*

To so experience Christ requires more than merely recognizing that we have many brothers and sisters here on earth. It necessitates acknowledging the on-going relationship we have with *all* the members of God's family, including our elder brothers and sisters in heaven. We not only find sure and heroic models for living out our faith, but also our strongest and most efficacious prayer partners. The saints in heaven—perfected in the love of Christ—are free from all selfish concerns. Liberated from the constraints of mortal flesh, they are tireless in their solicitude. Having come through the trials of this life, they wear the victor's crown and are arrayed in white robes of purity (cf. Revelation 2:10 and 6:11). As a result, they are able to intercede for us with a potency unmatched by those of us still beset by the weaknesses of this life.

St. Paul often directs all Christians to intercede for each other and the entire world (cf. 1 Timothy 2:1ff). Are we to believe that only the saints on earth are so bound? Would not charity dictate that the saints in heaven continue to intercede before the throne of Grace? St. James tells us, "The effective prayer of a righteous man can accomplish much" (James 5:16). If that is true for righteous men on earth, than how much more for those who have completed the journey of faith and are now forever perfected in the righteousness of Christ?

Herein we see the beautiful familial dimension of God's economy of salvation. While He desires all individuals to be saved, He does not save us as *isolated* individuals. He saves us as members of a body: the Body of Christ (cf. 1 Corinthians 12:27 and Ephesians 5:23). While we all must run the race set before us, we do not run it alone. We are quite literally surrounded by a great *"cloud of witnesses"* (Hebrews 12:1). This cloud of witnesses is composed of our elder brothers and sisters who have gone before us. They encourage us by their own examples and strengthen us by their ceaseless prayers on our behalf. They stand at the finish line cheering us on, more desirous for our final victory than even we are ourselves. Unlike us, they are no longer subject to the weaknesses and limitations of the flesh. They know what awaits us on the side. What we hope for in faith, they experience as reality.

But the familial dimension of God's plan does not stop here. In addition to having God as our Father and other Christians as our siblings, we have a spiritual *mother* as well. Catholic Christians regard the Blessed Virgin Mary as their spiritual mother and accordingly have a great devotion to her. This aspect of Catholic faith and practice is often a cause for great concern among Protestants. Generally speaking, they insist that the entire concept is foreign to the Scriptures and detracts from the unique prerogatives of Christ. Nothing could be further from the truth.

The Bible implicitly bears witness to Mary's maternal bond with all Christians by revealing to us our relationship to Jesus Christ. We are, as Scripture teaches, the brethren of Christ (Hebrews 2:10-17). It is the experience common to all humanity that those who are brethren have both a father and a mother in common. If we are the brothers and sisters of the Lord, His mother is our mother. This is born out beautifully at the foot of the Cross. It was there, at Calvary, in the midst of His Passion and suffering, that Jesus gave to the "Beloved Disciple" the exquisite gift of His very own mother (John 19:26-27). It is often assumed that Jesus was merely assuring provision for His mother. But this assumption ignores the tremendous gift being bestowed upon "the disciple whom Jesus loved." Though this disciple is traditionally recognized to be St. John the Evangelist, it is also traditionally recognized that the descriptive, "disciple whom Jesus loved," permits for the broader understanding of all disciples of Jesus Christ (for He loves them all) personified by St. John. Notice also that Jesus did not say, "Take care of *My* mother." Rather, He said, "Behold, *thy* mother." The beauty of what follows is often obscured by faulty translations. Verse 27 literally says, "And from that hour he took her as his own." The word "home" is not in the original Greek. It is merely assumed by the translators. However, this assumption waters down the full effect of the Greek: The beloved disciple took Mary as his own mother (as Catholic disciples of Jesus have ever since).

Later in this same disciple's life, he would see the mother of Jesus in his vision of the Apocalypse (the Book of Revelation). Therein he would refer to the fact that the Woman who bore the Savior would have many other children, namely, those "who keep the commandments of God and bear testimony to Jesus" (Revelation 12:1-6,17). In other words, Christians, or those who "hold to the testimony of Jesus," are sons and daughters of Mary.

Some may argue that "the Woman" is symbolic of Israel or the Church, and not Mary. While both Old Testament Israel and the New Testament Church are alluded to in the imagery, it is Mary who embodies "the Woman" in a complete and superlative way.

Does any of this detract from Christ? No. For one thing, it was *Jesus* who gave us His very mother to be our own. Mary's significance to us is inextricably bound to Christ. It is expressly because she is the Mother of Christ, who is our Brother, that we love her as our spiritual mother. The Incarnate Christ is the source and center of our relationship to Mary and to each other. It is really that simple. Yet, as simple and natural as it may seem to me now, the familial dimension to the walk of faith was somewhat blurred when I was a non-Catholic Christian. Now as a Catholic Christian, the experience of *Christ in the fullness of His family* has been brought into focus in a way that has, by God's grace, proven to be both beautiful and enriching.

# Chapter 17

# Christ in the Fullness of Vocation

How can I ever express the happiness of the marriage that is joined together by the Church, strengthened by an offering, sealed by a blessing, announced by angels, and ratified by the Father? How wonderful the bond between two believers, with a single hope, a single desire, a single observance, a single service! They are both brethren and both fellow servants; there is no separation between them in spirit or flesh. In fact they are truly two in one flesh, and where the flesh is one, one is the spirit (Tertullian).[23]

Throughout my years as a young adult Protestant, I struggled to discern God's call in my life. It was not until I came home to the Catholic Church, however, that I discovered my true *vocation* in life.

The *Catechism of the Catholic Church* defines "vocation" simply as "the calling or destiny we have in this life and hereafter."[24] It goes on to say that:

"God has created the human person to love and serve Him; the fulfillment of this vocation is eternal happiness. Christ calls the faithful to the perfection of holiness. The vocation of the laity consists in seeking the kingdom of God by engaging in temporal affairs and directing them according to God's will. Priestly and religious vocations are dedicated to the service of the Church as the universal sacrament of salvation."[25]

In other words, we are all, every single one of us, called "to know, love, and serve God in this life and to be happy with Him forever in the next."[26] This vocation is given an expressly Christian character by virtue of our baptism. Through baptism we become members of the Body of Christ and are called to holiness. We answer the call to holiness by cooperating with God's grace as He works to conform us to the image of Christ, culminating in our eternal union with the Most Holy Trinity. This is the vocation common to *all* Christians. We each, however, live out this baptismal vocation in what may be described as our *personal* or *particular* vocation. This particular vocation can take the form of a vocation to the priesthood or religious life, to consecrated singleness, or the married life. God calls us individually to that state of life wherein we can best serve Him and fulfill our baptismal vocation. In other words, our personal vocations are pathways to sanctity through which we come to know, love, serve, and glorify God.

For most of us, the particular vocation to which we are called is that of holy matrimony. When Gloria and I exchanged wedding vows in 1986, however, we did not have a *vocational* understanding of marriage. To be sure, we knew that we were embarking on a holy undertaking, for we recognized that marriage was ordained by God and intended by Him to reflect the love between Christ and His Church (Ephesians 5:31-32). But I cannot say that we saw marriage as a *calling* or a pathway to sanctification (the elements of vocation) and an actual channel of divine grace (something sacramental in nature). We recognized a divine dimension to Christian marriage, but we were unsure as to how that divine dimension is to be experienced in practical terms. As a result, we made a subtle, subconscious distinction between the work of our newly formed family and "the work of the Lord." Like many Protestants, we understood "the Lord's work" and His "call" as something external to the home.

I am reminded of an example that concerned the "Discipling Movement" within the Stone-Campbell Churches of Christ. This movement, also known as the "Crossroads Movement" or the "Boston Movement," was known for its zealous affirmation that to be a *true* Christian one must be a dedicated *disciple*. It emphasized personal Bible study and personal evangelism as indicators of whether or not one was truly a disciple of Christ, and, hence, a true Christian. While there is certainly merit to the connection between being a Christian and being a disciple (cf. Acts 11:26), the outworking of this principle within the movement often presented a skewed perception of discipleship. One congregation with which Gloria and I served was deeply influenced by this movement. As a result, some members seemed to approve of young mothers leaving their children with baby sitters in order to engage in "evangelism." In other words, their concept of evangelism was defined by certain activities that took place *outside* the home instead of seeing that the work of the home itself constituted an evangelistic witness to the faith.

The Catholic teaching on the vocation of marriage is often misunderstood. One such misconception is that the Catholic Church has a low view of marriage since she requires priests of the Latin rite to be celibate.* Nothing could be further from the

---

* Many non-Catholics even attempt to connect this discipline of the Church with the words of St. Paul in 1 Timothy 4:1-5 regarding false teachers who would espouse "doctrines of demons" by "forbid(ing) marriage and enjoining abstinence from foods." St. Paul here, however, is warning against various Gnostic heretics who regarded the material world itself as evil and, as a result, denigrated marriage and even practiced ritual starvation. The Catholic practice of priestly celibacy, on the other hand, is not rooted in a contempt for marriage but rather in the example of Christ. Moreover, it should be noted that the requirement of priestly celibacy is not absolute. Married men can be ordained to the priesthood in the Eastern rites of the Catholic Church, and several hundred married ex-Protestant clergy have been ordained to the Roman Catholic priesthood. A good source for information on the practice of priestly celibacy is *The Apostolic Origins of Priestly Celibacy* by Christian Cochini (San Francisco/Diego: Ignatius Press, 1990).

truth. In this regard, the *Catechism of the Catholic Church* cites the fourth-century Eastern Father and Doctor of the Church, St. John Chrysostom:

> Whoever denigrates marriage also diminishes the glory of virginity. Whoever praises it makes virginity more admirable and resplendent. What appears good only in comparison with evil would not be particularly good. It is something better than what is admitted to be good that is the most excellent good.[27]

In other words, the personal sacrifice made by those called to a life of consecrated virginity is an offering pleasing to God precisely *because* marriage is good. In fact, the Catholic Church teaches that Christian marriage is more than simply good, it is a *sacrament* and, as such, an actual vehicle of grace in the lives of spouses.[28]

The Church teaches that our Lord raised Christian marriage to the dignity of a sacrament precisely because the dignities and the duties of the vocation to holy matrimony *necessitate* it. The spousal covenant is, by God's design, one that is perpetual, indissoluble, and ordered to the mutual good of the spouses and the begetting and education of children.[29] To be faithful to such a calling, married couples need supernatural assistance. They need the special graces conferred by the sacrament.

Another area of misunderstanding involves the Catholic teaching on contraception (i.e., "birth control"). While it is fairly common knowledge that the Catholic Church forbids the use of contraceptives, the reasons for this stance are less widely known or understood. The Catholic teaching is rooted firmly in the natural moral law and the two-fold purpose of marriage. By natural moral law, the Church is referring to "the original moral sense which enables man to discern by reason the good and the evil, the truth and the lie."[30] Human reason alone is capable of recognizing and acknowledging the natural, divinely ordained connection between sexuality and procreation. This connection is given expression in the institution of marriage.

While all Christians unquestioningly acknowledge the first end of marriage, or "the good of the spouses," it would seem that not all recognize the second, which is the procreation and education of children. To be sure, it is assumed that most couples will *want* to have children and that they *will* have children. Protestants, however, by and large do not consider the intention to bear children a prerequisite for contracting Christian marriage. To conceive or not to conceive is almost universally regarded as strictly a matter of personal preference. When Gloria and I married, we definitely intended to have children, but we did not consider that intention an essential element of our marital covenant. To our way of thinking, this was optional.

That being the case, we believed the use of contraceptives in family planning to be perfectly licit, even prudent. Conversely, I thought the Catholic proscription of contraception to be ludicrous and nothing more than a papal plot to ensure a burgeoning population of Catholics. Moreover, like many others who had not carefully examined the Church's teaching, I thought that the Catholic ban on contraception would surely drive a wedge between husband and wife, resulting in weakened marriages and unstable families. I was wrong. What I thought would drive a wedge between Gloria and me has instead proven to be an avenue of incredible blessing.

Gloria and I can both readily testify to the numerous blessings that have come to our marriage as a direct result of embracing God's plan for holy matrimony as the Catholic Church presents it. First and foremost, it has resulted in a deep appreciation for the God-given gift of human sexuality and the corresponding privilege of participating in His work of procreation. Consequently, parenthood has been elevated from a mere personal choice to a divine calling (a holy vocation). It has also resulted in a deeper respect for each other and the way God has made us man and woman. In turn, this deeper respect has nurtured a more profound experience of marital intimacy than we ever dreamed possible. Moreover, it has brought us the most sublime and awe-inspiring of gifts: *children*.

Our experience may seem surprising to many, because it is often assumed that the Catholic teaching on contraception is indicative of a posture that is against sex. This would be laughable except that so many people have bought into this notion. The truth is, however, that *no* church has a more dignified view of human sexuality than the Catholic Church. For example, the *Catechism* teaches,

> The acts in marriage by which the intimate and chaste union of the spouses takes place are noble and honorable; the truly human performance of these acts fosters the self-giving they signify and enriches the spouses in joy and gratitude.[31]

Such words hardly indicate an "anti-sex" posture. In fact, it is precisely *because* the Catholic Church has such a lofty view of human sexuality that she stands firmly opposed to contraception, sterilization, fornication, adultery, homosexual acts, and self-abuse. She respects the beauty and dignity of human sexuality when it is expressed according to the divine plan; something that contraception, by its very nature, does not do.

Take the word itself: *contra*-ception. The word literally denotes some form of action that works *against* conception. This brings out an important distinction in the Church's teaching, the distinction between contraception and natural family planning (NFP). This distinction is rooted in the fact that contraception—by definition—is "the artificial prevention of the fertilization of the human ovum,"[32] whereas NFP does not involve taking *any* direct action against conception. Contraception facilitates that which is against the natural moral order by enabling couples to engage in marital intimacy while taking deliberate steps to thwart one of its primary purposes: procreation. NFP, on the other hand, works within the framework of the natural order by simply recognizing the cyclic nature of a woman's fertility. If, for serious reasons, a couple needs to avoid or delay pregnancy, they can simply abstain from intimacy during the woman's fertile period. The key difference is the openness to life and the recognition of God's designs for marriage and human sexuality. The bottom line is that, whereas NFP respects God's design, contraception works against it.

Does this mean that the Church requires Catholics to have as many children as is physically possible? No. The Church acknowledges that there may be "just reasons" for spacing children or avoiding pregnancy.[33] These reasons might include the health of the woman or extreme financial stress as, for example, during periods of unemployment. Couples are admonished, however, to make certain that their motives are not rooted in selfishness. The vocation of marriage, therefore, has, as one of its primary purposes, the begetting and nurturing of children for the Kingdom of God. Consequently, couples must guard against the insidious materialism and egoism that pervade our society and pressure them to limit their families to one or two children so that parents can pursue career goals, personal pleasure, and financial gain.

Ironically, the very things that supposedly hold the promise of fulfillment, those things that tempt couples to truncate the size of their families, end up proving to be empty and disappointing. On the other hand, couples who work within the divine plan find themselves experiencing a joy and sense of purpose that no career or level of financial success can ever hope to give. Even Christian ministry—when it conflicts with the responsibilities that spouses have toward each other and their children as part of their marriage vocation—can become a source of sadness and disorder in the home.

Despite the beauty, benefits, and authority of the Church's moral teaching concerning contraception, polls indicate that most Catholics in America use contraception. There are *many* reasons for this, but two of the primary reasons are simply ignorance and misinformation. I know this to be true from personal conversations with Catholics who express disagreement with the Church's teachings on this subject. In almost every such conversation, after I have explained the teachings and the reasons for them, the person invariably responded, "Oh, I didn't know that" or "I had not looked at it that way before." Many Catholics think that the Church's teaching on the inviolability of the conscience means that they are free to use contraception if their own conscience permits it. This is not the case. While the Church teaches that no one can, in good faith, act *against* what his or her conscience indicates is wrong, it also teaches that the conscience must be properly formed, or *informed,* by the teaching of the Church, since the conscience *on its own* cannot determine the objective morality of an action.

Ironically many Catholics, including clergy, seem to think that this teaching of the Church is a barrier to conversion, and yet, it was this teaching that first led me to view the Catholic Church in a somewhat positive light.

Before entering the Catholic Church, I was unsettled and searching for my niche. I had been trained to do "*the Lord's work,*" and assumed I needed to be looking for something outside of the everyday walk of life into which I could pour myself. Even though I tried to be a good Christian husband and father, I often felt as if my family life and my "ministry" were at odds. Now, thanks be to God, I have the peace that comes from embracing God's plan for my life; embracing the true meaning and purpose of my state in life. The Catholic Church has shown me that anything I do that is part of fulling my vocation as a husband and father is, in the truest sense of the word, Christian *ministry*. Even my present occupation as a salesman is, by extension, a holy undertaking because it is an integral aspect of my marital vocation. Moreover, the Church has taught me that whatever Christian ministry

I engage in must also be in harmony with my vocation as husband and father.

When we first began to study the Catholic faith, Gloria and I had been married for eight years. We thought that our investigation of Catholic Christianity would consist primarily in weighing the evidence pertaining to various controversial doctrines and practices. We were a reasonably happy couple and considered our marriage to be a strong one. Therefore, we were taken completely by surprise when we found the Catholic faith bringing about an unexpected and beautiful transformation of our marriage. Now, enlightened by the divinely revealed teachings of the Catholic Church and strengthened with the graces supplied by the sacraments, we can humbly and thankfully affirm that we are free to be what God has called us to be. In His great mercy, we have come to know *Christ in the fullness of vocation.*

Chapter 18

# Christ in the Fullness of Salvation

*For the moment all discipline seems painful rather than*
*pleasant; later it yields the peaceful fruit of righteousness*
*to those who have been trained by it. Therefore, lift your*
*drooping hands and strengthen your weak knees, and*
*make straight paths for your feet, so that what is lame*
*may not be put out of joint but rather be healed. Strive*
*for peace with all men, and for the holiness without*
*which no one will see the Lord (Hebrews 12:11-14).*

As I bring my story to a close, I am mindful that, while as a Catholic Christian I truly have been given *Christ in His fullness*, I have, to my shame, failed to conform myself completely to that fullness. That which I treasure so much as a Catholic—Christ in the fullness of His Word, in the fullness of His Sacraments, in the fullness of worship, in the fullness of His family, and in the fullness of vocation—are all things that I find myself, at times, taking for granted and neglecting. Of course, I am not at all unique in this; it is the same for most of us. This underscores one more aspect of Christ's fullness that was, in a sense, foreign to me as a Protestant but has been brought to light by the Catholic faith: *Christ in the fullness of salvation.*

As the passage of Scripture cited above indicates, Christians are to "strive for...the holiness without which no one will see the Lord." Other translations tell us to "pursue" holiness. Either way, the message is clear that Christians (those who are *already* adopted sons and daughters of God as described in the immediate context) are to strive for, or pursue, something. That something is holiness. Moreover, from the wording of this charge, two things are immediately apparent: (1) holiness is not something Christians automatically possess, or else they would have no need to pursue it, and (2) unless they attain this holiness, they cannot see the Lord. Holiness, therefore, is not something that is superfluous but absolutely essential. In order to enter into heaven, one must be holy.

As a Protestant Christian, I was taught that the holiness essential to our salvation is something that is *imputed* to us by Christ at the moment we are justified by faith, and is possessed by everyone who is *truly* saved. To be a Christian is, by definition, to be holy in the eyes of God. Though there is a certain degree of truth in this idea, it represents an *incomplete* concept of holiness.

The root concept of holiness (or sanctity) is that of being *set apart*. Objects that are said to be "holy" are set apart for a special purpose in that they are not for common or profane use. When used in reference to people, holiness means that they have been set apart by God and are called to live according to that which is uncommon, to separate themselves from sin, in order that they might become more like God and live in eternal union with the One who is the source of all holiness.

In keeping with the teaching of Sacred Scripture, the Catholic Church recognizes that, in one sense, personal holiness is imputed while, in another sense, it is an ongoing process—the process called *sanctification*. It is a present reality for every Christian in this life, though not *fully* attained until the next.

For example, in Scripture we find Christians being referred to as holy in regard to the status they *already* have before God while, at the same time, being recipients of a call to actually *be* holy in conduct. St. Paul referred to both of these together in the opening lines of his first epistle to the Corinthians, where he addressed his recipients as "those sanctified in Christ Jesus, called to be saints" (1 Corinthians 1:2). The essence of the spiritual life is our ongoing response to the call to holiness and will not find its complete fulfillment until our final sanctification when we are eternally united with God. It is at that time that "we shall be like Him, for we shall see Him as he is" (1 John 3:2). Moreover, it is for this reason that "every one who thus hopes in Him purifies himself as He is pure" (1 John 3:3).

It is this understanding of holiness that forms the backdrop for what we read in Hebrews 12:14 with its call to strive "for the holiness without which no one will see the Lord." The holiness that is called for is not that of the imputed sanctified status that all Christians already possess by virtue of their baptism into Christ, or else the charge to "strive for" or "pursue" it would be nonsensical. Rather, it is that holiness of life that is made possible by grace and expressed concretely by the practice of virtue and the love of God above all else. Moreover, based upon the wording of the text, this must not only be pursued but *must* be attained if heaven is to be one's eternal home. Yet, how many Christians depart from this life having actually attained complete holiness in word, thought, and deed?

The inspired writer of the letter to the Hebrews tells us that we must *pursue* and *attain* holiness if we are to see the Lord. Yet when we take a good, honest look at ourselves, we see within us the ugly vestiges of lust, pride, and sloth. We find that a distorted self-love still too often crowds out love for Christ. Even when our lives are marked by decades of progress in the spiritual life, self-examination reveals that we still are not as holy as we *can* be and, by implication, *ought* to be.

Where, then, does that leave us in regard to the absolute necessity of attaining holiness? How will we who are *imperfectly* holy be made *perfectly* holy between the moment when we draw our last breath in this life and our entering through the pearly gates of heaven?

In a word, we need *purgation*. We need a cleansing by which the dross of sinful attachments and disordered self-love is removed from us and our souls are made truly and actually holy as opposed to being merely *declared* holy. St. Paul referred to this cleansing also in his first epistle to the Corinthians:

> For no other foundation can any one lay than that which is laid, which is Jesus Christ. Now if any one builds on the foundation with gold, silver, precious stones, wood, hay, straw—each man's work will become manifest; for the Day will disclose it, because it will be revealed with fire, and the fire will test what sort of work each one has done. If the work which any man has built on the foundation survives, he will receive a reward. If any man's work is burned up, he will suffer loss, though he himself will be saved, but only as through fire.

The Catholic Church refers to this purifying process as *Purgatory*.

It is difficult to name a subject that is more consistently misunderstood than that of the Catholic teaching concerning Purgatory. It is important, therefore, that we consider both what Purgatory *is* and what it is *not*.

Regarding what Purgatory *is*, the *Catechism of the Catholic Church* presents the following:

> All who die in God's grace and friendship, but still imperfectly purified, are indeed assured of their eternal salvation; but after death they undergo purification, so as to achieve the holiness necessary to enter the joy of heaven. The Church gives the name Purgatory to this final purification of the elect, which is entirely different from the punishment of the damned.[34]

Note that Purgatory is defined as a purification process for *"all who die in God's grace and friendship."* It is strictly and exclusively for those who are *saved*. Additionally, the *Catechism* emphasizes the distinction between Purgatory and the punishment of the damned: they are "entirely different," in subject, nature, and purpose.

This, then, serves also to underscore what Purgatory is *not*: it is *not* a "second chance" extended to lost souls after death. In keeping with the teaching of Sacred Scripture, that "it is appointed for men to die once and after that comes judgment" (Hebrews 9:27), the Catholic Church teaches that, "Death puts an end to human life as the time open to either accepting or rejecting the divine grace manifested in Christ."[35] In regard to those who die in a lost condition, the Church affirms that "immediately after death the souls of those who die in a state of mortal sin descend into hell, where they suffer the punishments of hell."[36]

Purgatory, though certainly not a "second chance" for salvation, is the final application of the full benefits of the salvation that has been won by Christ for those who pass from this life in His friendship.

It should be noted that in making reference to the "state of mortal sin," the *Catechism* is employing terminology to which most Protestant Christians are not accustomed. We would do well to pause, therefore, and consider what the Church means by the term "mortal sin" and the corresponding teaching regarding the temporal and eternal consequences of mortal sin.

It is common knowledge that the Catholic Church has always made a distinction between sins based upon their gravity and their corresponding consequences. That distinction is expressed by the designations *mortal* and *venial*. As the *Catechism* states, "Mortal sin destroys charity in the heart of man by a grave violation of God's law; it turns man away from God, who is his ultimate end and his beatitude, by preferring an inferior good to him" whereas "venial sin allows charity to subsist even though it offends and wounds it."[37]

The term *"venial"* is derived from the Latin *venia* or pardon. It is referred to as such "because the soul still has the vital principle that allows a cure from within, similar to the healing of a sick or diseased body whose source of animation (the soul) is still present to restore the ailing bodily function to health."[38] In other words, mortal sin actually destroys supernatural life in the soul causing one to fall from grace, whereas venial sin—while not *destroying* supernatural life in the soul—*weakens* that life, thereby *predisposing* one to mortal sin.

Both as a Baptist and as a member of the Stone-Campbell Churches of Christ, I believed that sin was sin. I did not recognize any differentiation between sins that are venial and those that are mortal. In my mind, such a distinction was "unbiblical" and made light of the seriousness of *all* sin. Yet, it is in the Bible itself that we find just such a distinction. Consider the following words from St. John:

> If any one sees his brother committing what is not a mortal sin, he will ask, and God will give him life for those whose sin is not mortal. There is sin which is mortal; I do not say that one is to pray for that. All wrongdoing is sin, but there is sin which is not mortal (1 John 5:16-17).

Notice that St. John tells us that there is sin that is *mortal,* or literally *"unto death,"* and there is sin that is *not mortal* or, again, literally *"not unto death."* As a Church of Christ minister, I used to teach that this passage of Scripture was not so much making a distinction between sins *per se* as between individuals and their relationship to Christ at the time when they sin. In other words, sins committed while one was "walking in the light" (cf. 1 John 1:7) were automatically washed away by the blood of Jesus, whereas if one ever ceased to walk in the light, he was by definition walking in the darkness and his sins were *"unto* (or facing) *death.*" In this sense, I had learned and repeated the expression that "it is the *direction*, not the *perfection*, of your life that matters." This approach, however, completely overlooked the fact that the Apostle does not allow any middle ground. In other words, if one is walking with Christ in the light, a definitive act of turning around is required in order to begin walking in the darkness; there is a point at which one definitively changes direction. That definitive act is what the Catholic Church and St. John refer to as "mortal sin." If a Christian is walking in the light but then freely chooses to do something that he knows is gravely sinful, he has by definition committed a mortal sin and, as a consequence, has ceased to walk in the light. If, however, while walking in the light he sins in such a way that is either not grave in matter or not freely chosen with clear understanding, his sin is (as St. John would say) "*not mortal*" and he is still in the light. Hence, while "all wrongdoing is sin; there is sin that is not mortal."

This distinction between mortal and venial is necessary not only for the sake of accuracy in moral theology but in order to avoid distorting God's justice. There *are* sins that are truly damnable. They are the sins that are *freely* embraced even though the person committing them *knows* them to be grave offenses against God's moral law. They are what the Church refers to as *mortal* sins, and if not repented of, they result in eternal damnation. On the other hand, sins cannot rightly be termed *mortal* if they are either not serious in terms of their matter or, if serious, are either not known by the individual to be seriously sinful or are engaged in with some impediment to free will. In this case, the individual has not deliberately sinned so as to destroy the supernatural life of grace in the soul, and, therefore, has not completely severed his communion with God. These are referred to as *venial sins.*

By way of example, consider the heart-rending scenario of a teenage girl being coerced into having an abortion. While the

actual matter involved (the taking of innocent human life) is
certainly *grave* (serious), the young girl may not fully realize
what she is doing due to the deceptive misinformation she has
been provided. At the same time her free will may be seriously
hindered by the pressure brought to bear upon her by family
members and friends. Both her lack of clear understanding and
the inability to act freely may serve to mitigate her personal guilt
in what would otherwise be a mortal sin. Failure to recognize
such moral distinctions monstrously mutates both the perfect
justice and infinite mercy of God.

Does making such a distinction make light of venial sins?
Hardly. The Church has always insisted that even venial sins
should be taken seriously because by their very nature they
weaken us and predispose us to committing mortal sins. The
point, again, is that made by St. John: *"All wrongdoing is sin,
but there is sin which is not mortal."*

Closely related to the purifying dimension of Purgatory
is that of *expiation*. Expiation means "atonement for some
wrongdoing" which "implies an attempt to undo the wrong
that one has done, by suffering a penalty, by performing
a penance, or by making reparation or redress."[39] The
expiation accomplished in Purgatory concerns the *temporal*
punishment that is associated with venial sin and forgiven
mortal sin.

Protestant Christians are often taken aback by the
suggestion that there is some form of punishment due to sin that
Christians must undergo. They fear that such an idea denies the
"finished work of Christ" (cf. John 19:30). However, there is no
contradiction between the Catholic Church's view of Purgatory
and the fact that Christ has fully accomplished the work of our
redemption. But the question is, how is His work *applied* to our
souls? In other words, it is not a question of completion but of
application. After all, does not St. John tell us that Jesus "is the

expiation for our sins, and not for ours only but also for the sins of the whole world" (1 John 2:2)? St. Paul warns the Galatian Christians:

> Do not be deceived; God is not mocked, for whatever a man sows, that he will also reap. For he who sows to his own flesh will from the flesh reap corruption; but he who sows to the Spirit will from the Spirit reap eternal life (Galatians 6:7-8).

This warning, given to *Christians*, is utterly meaningless if a Christian does not suffer temporal punishment for sin. In other words, there is one sense in which Christ expiates our sins and another sense in which we ourselves expiate (pay a penalty for) our sins. That difference is the distinction that is properly made between the *eternal* consequences of our sins and the *temporal* consequences of our sins.

The eternal consequence for mortal sin is *death*. St. Paul calls such *"the wages of sin"* (Romans 6:23). While physical death is certainly in the picture, physical death is but an object lesson that points to something far more terrible, namely, eternal spiritual death (everlasting self-exclusion from communion with God and the life that He gives). Since this consequence is *eternal* in nature, it can be expiated only by an act of *infinite* value. That act of infinite value was, and is, the self-sacrifice of the sinless Son of God on the cross of Calvary. Jesus alone is capable of paying the *eternal* consequence of our sin and it is in *that* sense that He—*and He alone*—is "the expiation for our sins." However, even when we avail ourselves of the saving merits of Christ's atoning sacrifice, there remain the temporal consequences of our sin.

The temporal consequences of sin refer to that punishment due to sin that God's justice requires even though the sin has been forgiven and the *eternal* penalty paid for by Christ. It is punishment that lasts only for a time (the word "temporal" being derived from the Latin *tempus*, time). We see this punishment referred to in the verses immediately prior to the ones cited at the head of this chapter:

> My son, do not regard lightly the discipline of the Lord, nor lose courage when you are punished by Him. For the Lord disciplines him whom He loves, and chastises every son whom He receives (Hebrews 12:5-6, citing Proverbs 3:11-12).

Moreover, the inspired writer goes on to say that this discipline is given "for our good, that we may share in his holiness" (Hebrews 12:10). In other words, that very holiness for which we must strive and attain, if we are to *"see the Lord,"* is the direct result of our cooperation with the loving chastisement by which the Father disciplines us. The question, then, is why must we be chastised and disciplined? Is it not because we sin and have disordered attachments?

In regard to sin, the Scriptures show us that *all* sin carries with it the debt of pain. Sin—*even when forgiven*—carries with it a debt of temporal punishment that we must endure. Nowhere is this made clearer than in the case of David after his sin with Bathsheba. In 2 Samuel 12:13-14 we are told that even though David was forgiven for the sins of adultery and murder, he still had temporal consequences to suffer. This ties in well with what we have already noted regarding St. Paul's warning to the Christians in Galatia, namely the principle of sowing and reaping. With that sacred admonition in mind, are we to believe that one who lives a mediocre Christian life and dies in the state of grace—but without having reaped the consequences of sowing to the flesh—will simply pass through the gates of heaven with a great sigh of relief? If so, then God's justice has indeed been mocked. St. Paul, however, assures us that "God is not mocked, for whatever a man sows that he will also reap." Notice that there is no proviso stating, "Unless, of course, one dies without having reaped what one has sown." The principle would demand that there be some means whereby one is able to expiate sin by suffering the temporal consequences it incurs *even after death.*

Two other passages of Scripture serve to illustrate this point. The first is 2 Maccabees 12:39-46.* Therein we find Judas Maccabeus taking up a collection for the express purpose of making a sin offering in Jerusalem for some of his compatriots who had fallen in battle. In doing so, he is said to have "made atonement for the dead, that they might be delivered from their sin." This passage of Scripture not only witnesses to the Jewish belief that one can suffer even after death because of the temporal consequences of sin, but also points to the fact that prayers and sacrifices for the dead are pleasing in God's sight and not without salutary effect.

The second passage of Scripture is Matthew 5:25-26, where Jesus tells us:

> Make friends quickly with your accuser, while you are going with him to court, lest your accuser hand you over to the judge, and the judge to the guard, and you be put in prison; truly I say to you, you will never get out till you have paid the last penny.

With these words, Jesus is not merely offering sage advice about how to live prudently in this world. There is a spiritual application as well that speaks in principle to the present subject. In what sense can we be subjected to a prison sentence that is related to a debt that we owe and must pay? Moreover, our Lord indicates that those so consigned to debtors' prison can and will pay their debts and, subsequently, be released. It is the realities of the temporal punishment due to sin and the existence of Purgatory that provide clarity in regard to this otherwise strange admonition.

---

* Though Protestants generally do not regard *2 Maccabees* as canonical Scripture, the earliest Christians on record did. This is addressed in more detail in Appendix B.

So we have seen that the justice of God requires that we make restitution by suffering the temporal punishment due to venial sin and forgiven mortal sin. There is yet another aspect to this picture. As mentioned earlier, chastisement and discipline are made necessary by the twofold reality of our sin and our disordered attachments. If it is the justice of God that requires us to face the debt of temporal punishment due to sin, it is the mercy of God that brings us the discipline whereby our disordered attachments are severed and holiness of life made truly possible. Nonetheless, this merciful and loving discipline is said to be "painful" (Hebrews 12:11). It is through suffering that we are perfected in Christ.

All too often the beautiful reality of Christ's suffering on our behalf is distorted by the notion that Jesus suffered for us in order that we ourselves might *avoid* suffering. Nothing could be further from the truth. While it is true that our Lord's sufferings make it possible for us to avoid the suffering of eternal damnation, it is *not* true that His sufferings remove from us both the obligation and the need to suffer if we are to follow in His steps. St. Peter tells us, "To this you have been called, because Christ also suffered for you, leaving you an example, that you should follow in His steps" (1 Peter 2:21). Moreover, Jesus himself speaks of discipleship in terms of taking up our cross (Luke 9:23). It is impossible to follow Jesus and not endure suffering. What is more, St. Paul tells us that suffering with Christ is essential to our eternal salvation. He said we are "fellow heirs with Christ, provided we suffer with him in order that we may also be glorified with him" (Romans 8:17).

It would be a mistake to limit our suffering with Christ to simply that suffering which comes from persecution or the sacrifices we make in order to further the Gospel. There is also that suffering which we must endure if we are to grow in holiness. Our struggles against temptation involve real suffering, all the more so when we are beset by sinful habits and disordered attachments. It is this type of suffering that we find spoken of in the passage of Scripture cited at the beginning of this chapter (Hebrews 12:11-14). Sadly, it is also this type of suffering from which we so often shy away. Yet it is this very suffering—the suffering of divine chastening—that is necessary for attaining the holiness we need if we are to see the Lord and call heaven our home.

The Scriptures are plain enough. We *must* attain holiness if we are to be with God for all eternity, and holiness *requires* patiently enduring the suffering that must accompany the purifying discipline of God. Yet rare indeed are the Christians who fully embrace the cross and allow God to wholly sanctify them through holy suffering. What happens if, in this life, we shy away from the very thing that is necessary for our eternal beatitude? Are we cast into outer darkness because we fell somewhat short of allowing God to root out *all* vestiges of disordered attachments and distorted self-love from our hearts? God forbid! Thank God that, in his great mercy, He has made provision for our final and complete sanctification. That provision comes to us in the gift of Purgatory. Through the experience of Purgatory, God's justice is satisfied in regard to any unpaid debt of temporal punishment remaining from forgiven sins and God's mercy is known in the burning furnace of divine love that purges from us all disordered loves. In this way, we have the sure hope of experiencing *Christ in the fullness of salvation.*

# Epilogue

*"From his fullness have we all received, grace upon grace" (John 1:16).*

The process of writing this book has not been an easy task, for it has involved reawakening many precious and sometimes painful memories. My upbringing as a Southern Baptist afforded me experiences that I will treasure all of my life, and my years as a Church of Christ member and minister were not at all unhappy ones. For this reason, reducing my conversion to the Catholic faith to writing has been a bittersweet experience. On the one hand, it has given me great joy to share with others what the Lord, in His mercy, has done for me. On the other hand, my heart has been made heavy by recalling the many treasured relationships that have been strained, if not completely shattered, by my decision to become Catholic. At times I could almost wish that none of this had ever happened. But, thanks be to God, it did.

I say this because not all of my memories are pleasant ones. It is not pleasant to recall the uneasiness that resulted from denying papal infallibility while yearning for the certitude that only it could bring. I do not relish recalling the feelings of hopelessness and near despair resulting from my struggles against sin while not having access to the sacraments of Confession and Holy Communion. I am brought to shame upon remembering the many ways in which I failed Gloria and our children because of my inadequate understanding of the vocation of marriage. It is for these reasons, and so many more, that I can honestly say that my heart overflows with gratitude to our good God for giving to me *Christ in His fullness* through full incorporation into His Body, the Catholic Church.

> "Now to Him who by the power at work within us is able to do far more abundantly than all that we ask or think, to Him be glory in the church and in Christ Jesus to all generations, for ever and ever. Amen" (Ephesians 3:20-21).

Appendix A

# Early Christian Beliefs

Many non-Catholic Christians assume that the beliefs of the early Christians correspond with their own. They naturally like to think that the great saints and martyrs of the early Church were their forebears and kindred spirits. Likewise, they are generally of the persuasion that most Catholic doctrines blatantly contradict Scripture. In fact, Anti-Catholic polemicists typically claim that the Catholic Church *invented* most—*if not all*—of her distinctive teachings over a period of several hundred years.

I have seen "factual" chronologies of "Catholic Inventions" that provide dates for when various Catholic beliefs were allegedly invented by the Church. One such list suggests that the belief in Purgatory was an not established doctrine until A.D. 593 and that the intercession of angels and saints was concocted around 600.[40] The same list goes on to imply that Extreme Unction (i.e., sacrament of Anointing the Sick) did not make its appearance until 526, and that Pope Innocent III invented both Transubstantiation (the belief in Christ's Real Presence in the Eucharist) and the Sacrament of Confession in the year 1215. Moreover, the same anti-Catholic writer goes on to state that the Catholic Church added the Deuterocanonical Books (i.e., the seven Old Testament books that are in Catholic Bibles but not in Protestant Bibles) in the year 1546 (this error is addressed in Appendix B).

This would all be pretty damaging to Catholic claims *if* it were true, but as the following citations will demonstrate, the dates are arbitrary and rooted more in bigotry than in scholarship.

The following citations are presented to demonstrate that authentic Catholic teaching, as explicated in the *Catechism of the Catholic Church (CCC)*, is reflected in the Sacred Scriptures, as the earliest Christians on record understood them. It is important to note that in citing the early Fathers of the Church, I am not placing the words of men over and above the Word of God. The Fathers are cited simply to show how the earliest Christians on record understood the teaching of Scripture and practiced the faith that they had received from the Apostles. Their writings demonstrate that they were not innovators. Rather, they fought to defend and preserve the Deposit of Faith as it had been delivered to them. In so doing, many of them made the supreme sacrifice of their lives.

The citations are arranged topically and are not intended to constitute an exhaustive treatment of any particular topic. Rather, they are intended to whet the appetite for further study (study that should include the books listed under Suggested Reading). While both the list of topics and the number of citations could be multiplied, the ones provided will suffice to demonstrate that the Catholic faith of today is the same faith witnessed to in the Scriptures and for which the early Christians gave their lives.

## Baptism is Necessary for Salvation

### Catholic Faith:

"The Lord himself affirms that baptism is necessary for salvation [John 3:5]...Baptism is necessary for salvation for those to whom the Gospel has been proclaimed and who have had the possibility of asking for this sacrament [Mark 16:16]" (*CCC* 1257).

### Teaching of Scripture:

"Jesus answered him, 'Truly, truly, I say to you, unless one is born anew, he cannot see the kingdom of God.' Nicodemus said to him,

'How can a man be born when he is old? Can he enter a second time into his mother's womb and be born?' Jesus answered, 'Truly, truly, I say to you, unless one is born of water and the Spirit, he cannot enter the kingdom of God (John 3:3-5).'"*

"And he said to them, 'Go into all the world and preach the gospel to the whole creation. He who believes and is baptized will be saved; but he who does not believe will be condemned'" (Mark 16:15-16).**

"And now why do you wait? Rise and be baptized, and wash away your sins, calling on his name." (Acts 22:16)

## Early Christian Testimony:

"'I have heard, sir,' said I [to the Shepherd], 'from some teachers, that there is no other repentance except that which took place when we went down into the water and obtained the remission of our former sins.' He said to me, 'You have heard rightly, for so it is'" (**Hermas**, *The Shepherd* 4:3:1–2 [J-87] [A.D. 80]).

"Whoever is convinced and believes that what they are taught and told by us is the truth, and professes to be able to live accordingly...are led by us to a place where there is water; and there they are reborn in the same kind of rebirth in which we ourselves were reborn: in the name of God, the Lord and Father of all, and of our Savior, Jesus Christ, and of the Holy Spirit, they receive the washing with water. For Christ said, 'Unless you be reborn, you shall not enter into the kingdom of heaven'" (**Justin Martyr**, *First Apology* 61 [J-126] [A.D. 151]).

---

* Jesus parallels the new birth of verse three with being "born of water and the Spirit" in verse five.

** Jesus plainly states that to be saved, one must both believe and be baptized. The fact that he does not mention Baptism in the subsequent phrase ("he who does not believe will be condemned") does not change what he said about the necessity of Baptism. For one who has attained the age of reason, Baptism apart from faith is worthless.

# The Sacrament of Confession[*]

## Catholic Faith:

Christ instituted the sacrament of Penance for all sinful members of his Church: above all for those who, since Baptism, have fallen into grave sin, and have thus lost their baptismal grace and wounded ecclesial communion. It is to them that the sacrament of Penance offers a new possibility to convert and to recover the grace of justification. The Fathers of the Church present this sacrament as "the second plank [of salvation] after the shipwreck which is the loss of grace" (*CCC* 1446).

## Teaching of Scripture:

"Jesus said to them again, 'Peace be with you. As the Father has sent me, even so I send you.' And when he had said this, he breathed on them, and said to them, 'Receive the Holy Spirit. If you forgive the sins of any, they are forgiven; if you retain the sins of any, they are retained'" (John 20:21-23).

## Early Christian Testimony:

"Confess your offenses in church, and do not go up to your prayer with an evil conscience...On the Day of the Lord gather together, break bread and give thanks, after confessing your transgressions so that your sacrifice may be pure" (*Didache* 4:14, 14:1 [J-3 & J-8] [A.D. 70]).

"Then one of the bishops present shall, at the request of all, impose his hand on the one who is being ordained bishop, and shall pray thus, saying: 'God and Father of our Lord Jesus Christ...pour forth now that power which comes from you, from your Royal Spirit, which you gave to your Beloved Son Jesus Christ and which He bestowed upon His holy Apostles...grant to this your servant, whom you have chosen for the episcopate, to feed your holy flock

---

[*] Also called the Sacrament of Penance and the Sacrament of Reconciliation.

and to serve without blame as your high priest, ministering night and day to propitiate unceasingly before your face; and to offer to you the gifts of your holy Church; and by the Spirit of the high-priesthood to have the authority to forgive sins, in accord with your command" (**St**. **Hippolytus of Rome**, *Apostolic Tradition* 3 [J-394a] [A.D. 215]).

"The Apostle likewise bears witness and says, 'You cannot drink the cup of the Lord and the cup of devils...Whoever eats the Bread or drinks the Cup of the Lord unworthily will be guilty of the Body and Blood of the Lord.' But they spurn and despise all these warnings; and before their sins are expiated, before they have made a confession of their crime, before their conscience has been purged in the ceremony and at the hand of the priest... they do violence to His Body and Blood; and with their hands and mouth they sin against the Lord more than when they denied him" (**St. Cyprian of Carthage**, *The Lapsed* 15:1-3 (J-551) [A.D. 251]).

"Of how much greater faith and more salutary fear are they who... confess even this to the priests of God in a straightforward manner and in sorrow, making an open declaration of conscience...I beseech you, brethren, let everyone who has sinned confess his sin while he is still in this world, while his confession is still admissible, while satisfaction and remission made through the priests are still pleasing before the Lord" (ibid., 28, J-553).

# The Real Presence of Christ in the Eucharist

## Catholic Faith:

"At the heart of the Eucharistic celebration are the bread and the wine that, by the words of Christ and the invocation of the Holy Spirit, become Christ's Body and Blood" (*CCC* 1333).

## Teaching of Scripture:

"'I am the living bread which came down from heaven; if any one eats of this bread, he will live for ever; and the bread which I shall give for the life of the world is my flesh.' The Jews then disputed among themselves, saying, 'How can this man give us his flesh to eat?' So Jesus said to them, 'Truly, truly, I say to you, unless you eat the flesh of the Son of man and drink his blood, you have no life in you; he who eats my flesh and drinks my blood has eternal life, and I will raise him up at the last day. For my flesh is food indeed, and my blood is drink indeed. He who eats my flesh and drinks my blood abides in me, and I in him'" (John 6:51-56).

"Now as they were eating, Jesus took bread, and blessed, and broke it, and gave it to the disciples and said, 'Take, eat; this is my body.' And he took a cup, and when he had given thanks he gave it to them, saying, 'Drink of it, all of you; for this is my blood of the new covenant, which is poured out for many for the forgiveness of sins'" (Matthew 26:26-28).

"The cup of blessing which we bless, is it not a participation in the blood of Christ? The bread which we break, is it not a participation in the body of Christ?" (1 Corinthians 10:16-17)

## Early Christian Testimony:

"Take note of those who hold heterodox opinions on the grace of Jesus Christ which has come to us, and see how contrary their opinions are to the mind of God...They abstain from the Eucharist and from prayer, because they do not confess that the Eucharist is the Flesh of our Savior Jesus Christ, Flesh which suffered for our sins and which the Father, in his goodness, raised up again (**St. Ignatius of Antioch**, *Letter to the Smyrneans* 6:2–7:1 [J-64] [A.D. 110]).

"We call this food Eucharist; and no one else is permitted to partake of it, except one who believes our teaching to be true and who has been washed in the washing which is for the remission of sins and for regeneration, and is thereby living as Christ has enjoined. For not as common bread nor common drink do we receive these; but since Jesus Christ our Savior was made incarnate by the word of God and had both flesh and blood for our salvation, so too, as we have been taught, the food which has been made into the Eucharist by the Eucharistic prayer set down by Him, and by the change of which our blood and flesh is nurtured, is both the flesh and the blood of that incarnated Jesus" (**St. Justin Martyr**, *First Apology* 66 [J-128] [A.D. 151]).

"He has declared the cup, a part of creation, to be his own Blood, from which he causes our blood to flow; and the bread, a part of creation, he has established as his own Body, from which he gives increase to our bodies. When, therefore, the mixed cup and the baked bread receives the Word of God and becomes the Eucharist, the Body of Christ, and from these the substance of our flesh is increased and supported, how can they say that the flesh is not capable of receiving the gift of God, which is eternal life—flesh which is nourished by the Body and Blood of the Lord, and is in fact a member of him?" (**St. Irenaeus of Lyon**, *Against Heresies* 5:2 [J-249][A.D. 189])

"I promised you, who have now been baptized, a sermon in which I would explain the Sacrament of the Lord's Table...That Bread which you see on the altar, having been sanctified by the word of God, is the Body of Christ. That chalice, or rather, what is in that chalice, having been sanctified by the word of God, is the Blood of Christ" (**St. Augustine of Hippo**, *Sermons* 227 [J-1519] [A.D. 411]).

# The Primacy of St. Peter and His Successors (the Bishops of Rome)*

## Catholic Faith:

"The Lord made Simon alone, whom he named Peter, the 'rock' of his Church. He gave him the keys of his Church and instituted him shepherd of the whole flock. 'The office of binding and loosing

* This topic is given special attention in Appendix H, *Peter and the Papacy.*

which was given to Peter was also assigned to the college of apostles united to its head.' This pastoral office of Peter and the other apostles belongs to the Church's very foundation and is continued by the bishops under the primacy of the Pope" (*CCC* 881).

## Teaching of Scripture:

"And I tell you, you are Peter, and on this rock I will build my church, and the powers of death shall not prevail against it. I will give you the keys of the kingdom of heaven, and whatever you bind on earth shall be bound in heaven, and whatever you loose on earth shall be loosed in heaven" (Matthew 16:18-19).

"When they had finished breakfast, Jesus said to Simon Peter, 'Simon, son of John, do you love me more than these?' He said to him, 'Yes, Lord; you know that I love you.' He said to him, 'Feed my lambs.' A second time he said to him, 'Simon, son of John, do you love me?' He said to him, 'Yes, Lord; you know that I love you.' He said to him, 'Tend my sheep.' He said to him the third time, 'Simon, son of John, do you love me?' Peter was grieved because he said to him the third time, 'Do you love me?' And he said to him, 'Lord, you know everything; you know that I love you.' Jesus said to him, 'Feed my sheep'" (John 21:15-17).

## Early Christian Testimony:

"Owing to the sudden and repeated calamities and misfortunes which have befallen us, we must acknowledge that we have been somewhat tardy in turning our attention to the matters in dispute among you, beloved; and especially that abominable and unholy sedition, alien and foreign to the elect of God, which a few rash and self-willed persons have inflamed to such madness that your venerable and illustrious name, worthy to be loved by all men, has been greatly defamed...Accept our counsel, and you will have nothing to regret...If anyone disobey the things which have been said by Him through us, let them know that they will involve themselves in transgression and in no small danger...You will afford us joy and gladness if, being obedient to the things which we have written through the Holy Spirit, you will root out the wicked passion of jealousy" (**St. Clement of Rome**, *Letter to the Corinthians* 1, 58–59, 63 [J-10a, 28, 28a, 29][A.D. 80]).*

"Ignatius...to the church also which holds the presidency in the place of the country of the Romans, worthy of God, worthy of honor, worthy of blessing, worthy of praise, worthy of success, worthy of sanctification, and, because you hold the presidency in love, named after Christ and named after the Father" (**St. Ignatius of Antioch**, *Letter to the Romans* 1:1 [J-52] [A.D. 110]).

"The blessed Apostles [Peter and Paul], having founded and built up the church [of Rome], they handed over the office of the episcopate to Linus" (**St. Irenaeus of Lyon**, *Against Heresies* 3:3:3 [J-211] [A.D. 189]).**

"[T]he blessed Peter, the chosen, the pre-eminent, the first among the disciples, for whom alone with Himself the Savior paid the tribute, quickly grasped and understood their meaning. And what does he say? 'Behold, we have left all and have followed you'" (**St. Clement of Alexandria**, *Who Is the Rich Man That Is Saved?* 21:3–5 [J-436] [A.D. 200]).

"The Lord says to Peter: 'I say to you,' He says, 'that you are Peter, and upon this rock I will build my Church'...On him He builds the Church, and to him He gives the command to feed the sheep; and although He assigns a like power to all the Apostles, yet He founded a single chair, and He established by His own authority a source and an intrinsic reason for that unity. Indeed, the others were that also which Peter was; but a primacy is given to Peter, whereby

---

* Clement, Bishop of Rome and successor of St. Peter, writes to the Corinthians claiming an authority that they apparently recognized (as did all of the churches). Note also that it has always been customary for popes to speak in the first person plural ("we") in formal communications. This is due to the fact that no pope is speaking merely as an individual. He is speaking for the Church. He is speaking in union with all of his predecessors (including St. Peter). Most importantly, he is speaking as the representative of Christ on earth.

** The Apostles had successors. In this case, Linus was appointed as the Bishop of Rome (the successor of St. Peter).

it is made clear that there is but one Church and one chair. So too, all are shepherds, and the flock is shown to be one, fed by all the Apostles in single-minded accord. If someone does not hold fast to this unity of Peter, can he imagine that he still holds the faith? If he desert the chair of Peter upon whom the Church was built, can he still be confident that he is in the Church?" (**St. Cyprian of Carthage**, *The Unity of the Catholic Church* 4; 1st edition [J-555 – 556] [A.D. 251])

"(T)hey have not the succession of Peter, who hold not the chair of Peter, which they rend by wicked schism; and this, too, they do, wickedly denying that sins can be forgiven even in the Church, whereas it was said to Peter: "I will give unto thee the keys of the kingdom of heaven, and whatsoever thou shalt bind on earth shall be bound also in heaven, and whatsoever thou shall loose on earth shall be loosed also in heaven." And the vessel of divine election himself said: "If ye have forgiven anything to any one, I forgive also, for what I have forgiven I have done it for your sakes in the person of Christ" (**St. Ambrose of Milan**, *On Penance*, Book One, Ch. VII, v. 33 [c. A.D. 390]).[42]

## Merit and Salvation

This particular area is quite often misunderstood by non-Catholics. Many Protestant Christians believe that the concept of meriting reward for good works is contrary to the Gospel message. They tend to think that the Catholic concept of merit amounts to an earning of one's salvation. Our Lord Jesus Christ taught, however, that we do indeed merit rewards for our service to Him. Moreover, the Church teaches that we *cannot* merit the initial grace of forgiveness and justification. Rather, it is subsequent to our initial justification that we can merit the additional graces we need to finish the course and attain eternal life. Such merit, however, is due strictly to cooperation with God's grace. Therefore, from start to finish our salvation is the work of God's grace.

## Catholic Faith:

"MERIT: The reward which God promises and gives to those who love him and by his grace perform good works" (CCC Glossary).

"With regard to God, there is no strict right to merit on the part of man. Between God and us there is an immeasurable inequality, for we have received everything from him, our Creator" (*CCC* 2007).

"The merit of man before God in the Christian life arises from the fact that *God has freely chosen to associate man with the work of his grace*" (*CCC* 2008).

"Since the initiative belongs to God in the order of grace, *no one can merit the initial grace* of forgiveness and justification, at the beginning of conversion. Moved by the Holy Spirit and by charity, *we can merit* for ourselves and for others the graces needed for our sanctification, for the increase of grace and charity, and for the attainment of eternal life" (*CCC* 2010).

## Teaching of Scripture:

"Do not lay up for yourselves treasures on earth, where moth and rust consume and where thieves break in and steal, but lay up for yourselves treasures in heaven, where neither moth nor rust consumes and where thieves do not break in and steal" (Matthew 6:19-20).

"For the Son of man is to come with His angels in the glory of His Father, and then He will repay every man for what he has done" (Matthew 16:27).

"For he will render to every man according to his works: to those who by patience in well-doing seek for glory and honor and immortality, he will give eternal life; but for those who are factious and do not obey the truth, but obey wickedness, there will be wrath and fury" (Romans 2:6-8).

## Early Christian Testimony:

"Be pleasing to Him whose soldiers you are, and whose pay you receive. May none of you be found to be a deserter. Let your Baptism be your armament; your faith, your helmet; your love, your spear; your endurance, your full suit of armor. Let your works be as your deposited withholdings, so that you may receive the back-pay which has accrued to you" (**St. Ignatius of Antioch**, *Letter to Polycarp* 6:2 [J-68] [A.D. 110]).

"We have learned from the Prophets and we hold it as true that punishments and chastisements and good rewards are distributed according to the merit of each man's actions" (**St. Justin Martyr**, *First Apology* 43 [J-123] [A.D. 151]).

"He who gave the mouth for speech and formed the ears for hearing and made eyes for seeing will examine everything and will judge justly, granting recompense to each according to merit. To those who seek immortality by the patient exercise of good works, he will give everlasting life, joy, peace, rest, and all good things, which has neither eye seen nor ear has heard, nor has it entered into the heart of man. For the unbelievers and the contemptuous, and for those who do not submit to the truth but assent to iniquity… there will be wrath and indignation [Rom. 2:8]" (**St. Theophilus of Antioch**, *To Autolycus* 1:14 [J-176] [A.D. 181]).

"[Paul], an able wrestler, urges us on in the struggle for immortality, so that we may receive a crown, and so that we may regard as a precious crown that which we acquire by our own struggle, and which does not grow upon us spontaneously…Those things which come to us spontaneously are not loved as much as those which are obtained by anxious care" (**St. Irenaeus of Lyon**, *Against Heresies* 4:37:7 [J-246] [A.D. 189]).

"We are commanded to live righteously, and the reward is set before us of our meriting to live happily in eternity. But who is able to live righteously and do good works unless he has been justified by faith?" (**St. Augustine of Hippo**, *Various Questions to Simplician* 1:2:21 [J-1575] [A.D. 396])

"What merit, then, does a man have before grace, by which he might receive grace, when our every good merit is produced in us only by grace, and, when God, crowning our merits, crowns nothing else but His own gifts to us?" (**St. Augustine of Hippo**, *Letters* 194:5:19 [J-1452] [A.D. 418])

# The Intercession of Angels & Saints in Heaven

## Catholic Faith:

"Being more closely united to Christ, those who dwell in heaven fix the whole Church more firmly in holiness…(T)hey do not cease to intercede with the Father for us, as they proffer the merits which they acquired on earth through the one mediator between God and men, Christ Jesus…So by their fraternal concern is our weakness greatly helped" (CCC 956).

## Teaching of Scripture:

"And when he had taken the scroll, the four living creatures and the twenty-four elders fell down before the Lamb, each holding a harp, and with golden bowls full of incense, which are the prayers of the saints" (Revelation 5:8).

"And another angel came and stood at the altar with a golden censer; and he was given much incense to mingle with the prayers of all the saints upon the golden altar before the throne; and the smoke of the incense rose with the prayers of the saints from the hand of the angel before God" (Revelation 8:3-4).

"See that you do not despise one of these little ones; for I tell you that in heaven their angels always behold the face of my Father who is in heaven" (Matthew 18:10).

"Therefore confess your sins to one another, and pray for one another, that you may be healed. The prayer of a righteous man has great power in its effects" (James 5:16).*

## Early Christian Testimony:

"But those who are weak and slothful in prayer, hesitate to ask anything from the Lord; but the Lord is full of compassion, and gives without fail to all who ask Him. But you, having been strengthened by the holy Angel, and having obtained from (H)im such intercession, and not being slothful, why do not you ask of the Lord understanding, and receive it from Him?" (**Shepherd of Hermas,** *The Shepherd* 3:5:4 [A.D. 80]).[45]

"So is he [the Christian] always pure for prayer. He also prays in the society of angels, as being already of angelic rank, and he is never out of their holy keeping; and though he pray alone, he has the choir of the saints standing with him [in prayer]" (**St. Clement of Alexandria,** *Miscellanies* 7:12 [A.D. 208]).[46]

"But these pray along with those who genuinely pray—not only the high priest but also the angels who 'rejoice in heaven over one repenting sinner more than over ninety-nine righteous that need not repentance,' and also the souls of the saints already at rest" (**Origen,** *On Prayer,* Ch. VI [A.D. 233]).[45]

"Let us on both sides always pray for one another. Let us relieve burdens and afflictions by mutual love, that if any one of us, by the swiftness of divine condescension, shall go hence the first, our love may continue in the presence of the Lord, and our prayers for our brethren and sisters not cease in the presence of the Father's mercy" (**St. Cyprian of Carthage,** *Letters* 56:5 [A.D. 253]).[46]

"Then we make mention of those who have already fallen asleep: first the patriarchs, prophets, Apostles, and martyrs, that through their prayers and supplications God would receive our petition" (**St. Cyril of Jerusalem,** *Catechetical Lectures* 23:9 [J-852] [A.D. 350]).

---

* If the prayers of those who are righteous here on earth have great power, then how much more so are the prayers of those who have been perfected in heaven?

## Final Purification (*Purgatory*)

Protestant Christians often reject Purgatory because they cannot find the word "Purgatory" in the Bible. However, by that same line of reasoning, they should not believe in the Holy Trinity either (for the word "Trinity" is not found in the Bible). Yet, to reject the Holy Trinity would be to reject the key mystery of Christianity. Therefore, the question is not one of *terminology* (whether or not a particular word is found in Sacred Scripture) but of *theology* (whether or not a particular concept is actually taught in Scripture). In that regard, as the following citations indicate, the concept of final purgation (Purgatory) is both rooted in the teachings of Sacred Scripture and witnessed to by the beliefs of the early Church.

### Catholic Faith:

"All who die in God's grace and friendship, but still imperfectly purified, are indeed assured of their eternal salvation; but after death they undergo purification, so as to achieve the holiness necessary to enter the joy of heaven" (*CCC* 1030).

"The Church gives the name *Purgatory* to this final purification of the elect, which is entirely different from the punishment of the damned" (*CCC* 1031).*

### Teaching of Scripture:

"And have you forgotten the exhortation which addresses you as sons?—'My son, do not regard lightly the discipline of the Lord, nor lose courage when you are punished by him. For the Lord disciplines him whom he loves, and chastises every son whom he receives.' It is for discipline that you have to endure. God

* The Church clearly teaches that Purgatory is not a "second chance" at salvation. It is only for those who die in the state of grace. Those who do not die in the state of grace (i.e., the damned) descend to hell immediately upon death (cf., *CCC* 1035).

is treating you as sons; for what son is there whom his father does not discipline? If you are left without discipline, in which all have participated, then you are illegitimate children and not sons. Besides this, we have had earthly fathers to discipline us and we respected them. Shall we not much more be subject to the Father of spirits and live? For they disciplined us for a short time at their pleasure, but he disciplines us for our good, that we may share his holiness. For the moment all discipline seems painful rather than pleasant; later it yields the peaceful fruit of righteousness to those who have been trained by it. Therefore lift your drooping hands and strengthen your weak knees, and make straight paths for your feet, so that what is lame may not be put out of joint but rather be healed. Strive for peace with all men, and for the holiness without which no one will see the Lord" (Hebrews 12:5-14).*

"Now if any one builds on the foundation with gold, silver, precious stones, wood, hay, stubble—each man's work will become manifest; for the Day will disclose it, because it will be revealed with fire, and the fire will test what sort of work each one has done. If the work which any man has built on the foundation survives, he will receive a reward. If any man's work is burned up, he will suffer loss, though he himself will be saved, but only as through fire" (1 Corinthians 3:12-15).**

"Make friends quickly with your accuser, while you are going with him to court, lest your accuser hand you over to the judge, and the judge to the guard, and you be put in prison; truly, I say

---

* The principle of chastisement and discipline coupled with the pursuit of holiness ("without which no one will see the Lord") is the very essence of the concept of purgatory.
** St. Paul speaks of the one who builds shabbily upon the foundation of Christ as suffering loss but being saved in the end. This "Day" of testing by fire is clearly either (1) at the end of time or (2) at the end of one's life. Either way, this suffering of loss on the part of the saved individual occurs after this life. It is unthinkable that there will be suffering in Heaven (i.e. even the suffering of loss). Therefore, it implies a testing and purgation process that occurs after this life but before one's entry into Heaven. Again, this is what the Catholic Church refers to as "Purgatory."

to you, you will never get out till you have paid the last penny"
(Matthew 5:25-26). *

"So they all blessed the ways of the Lord, the righteous Judge,
who reveals the things that are hidden; and they turned to prayer,
beseeching that the sin which had been committed might be wholly
blotted out. And the noble Judas exhorted the people to keep
themselves free from sin, for they had seen with their own eyes
what had happened because of the sin of those who had fallen.
He also took up a collection, man by man, to the amount of two
thousand drachmas of silver, and sent it to Jerusalem to provide
for a sin offering. In doing this he acted very well and honorably,
taking account of the resurrection. For if he were not expecting
that those who had fallen would rise again, it would have been
superfluous and foolish to pray for the dead. But if he was looking
to the splendid reward that is laid up for those who fall asleep in
godliness, it was a holy and pious thought. Therefore he made
atonement for the dead, that they might be delivered from their sin"
(2 Maccabees 12:41-46). **

## Early Christian Testimony:

"And after the exhibition, Tryphaena again receives her.
For her daughter Falconilla had died, and said to her in a
dream: Mother, thou shalt have this stranger Thecla in my
place, in order that she may pray concerning me, and that I
may be transferred to the place of the just (*Acts of Paul and
Thecla* [A.D. 160]).[47]

---

* The Sermon on the Mount is about salvation and living the Kingdom life, not about
how to stay out of earthly prison. Here He speaks of debts—spiritual debts—that we
must pay.
** The implication of the inspired writer's underscoring of the salutary nature of
prayers for the dead is that the dead can, in fact, benefit from such. Those in Heaven
have no need of our prayers; those in Hell cannot benefit from them. Therefore, it
points to a third, temporary state: what the Catholic Church refers to as "Purgatory".
This implication is so unavoidable that early Protestant leaders chose to remove the
Book of Second Maccabees from their Bibles (this is addressed in Appendix B).

"The citizen of a prominent city, I erected this while I lived, that I might have a resting place for my body. Abercius is my name, a disciple of the chaste shepherd who feeds His sheep on the mountains and in the fields, who has great eyes surveying everywhere, who taught me the faithful writings of life...Standing by, I, Abercius, ordered this to be inscribed; Truly, I was in my seventy-second year. May everyone who is in accord with this and who understands it pray for Abercius" (*Epitaph of Abercius* [J-187] [A.D. 190])."

"We offer sacrifices for the dead on their birthday anniversaries" (**Tertullian**, *The Crown* 3:3 [ J-367] [A.D. 211])."

"The strength of the truly believing remains unshaken; and with those who fear and love God with their whole heart, their integrity continues steady and strong. For to adulterers even a time of repentance is granted by us, and peace [i.e., reconciliation] is given. Yet virginity is not therefore deficient in the Church, nor does the glorious design of continence languish through the sins of others. The Church, crowned with so many virgins, flourishes; and chastity and modesty preserve the tenor of their glory. Nor is the vigor of continence broken down because repentance and pardon are facilitated to the adulterer. It is one thing to stand for pardon, another thing to attain to glory; it is one thing, when cast into prison, not to go out thence until one has paid the uttermost farthing; another thing at once to receive the wages of faith and courage. It is one thing, tortured by long suffering for sins, to be cleansed and long purged by fire; another to have purged all sins by suffering. It is one thing, in fine, to be in suspense till the sentence of God at the day of judgment; another to be at once crowned by the Lord" (**St. Cyprian of Carthage**, *Letters* 51[55]:20 [A.D. 253]).

"(N)ext, we make mention also of the holy fathers and bishops who have already fallen asleep, and, to put it simply, of all among us who have already fallen asleep, for we believe that it will be of very

---

* This Christian epitaph is an explicit acknowledgment of the need for prayers after death (i.e., because of the existence of an intermediary place of purgation).
** In other words, sacrifices were offered on the anniversary of the departed one's death (i.e., the birthday into eternal life).

great benefit to the souls of those for whom the petition is carried up, while this holy and most solemn sacrifice is laid out" (**St. Cyril of Jerusalem**, *Catechetical Lectures* 23:5:9 [J-852] [A.D. 350]).*

"There is an ecclesiastical discipline, as the faithful know, when the names of the martyrs are read aloud in that place at the altar of God, where prayer is not offered for them. Prayer, however, is offered for other dead who are remembered. For it is wrong to pray for a martyr, to whose prayers we ought ourselves be commended" (**St. Augustine of Hippo**, *Sermons* 159:1 [J-1513] [A.D. 411]).**

"Temporal punishments are suffered by some in this life only, by some after death, by some both here and hereafter; but all of them before that last and strictest judgement. But not all who suffer temporal punishments after death will come to eternal punishments, which are to follow after that judgment" (St. Augustine of Hippo, *The City of God*, 21, 13 [J-1776] [inter. A.D. 413-426]).

---

* St. Cyril not only bears witness to prayers for the dead but to the fact that the sacrifice of the Mass was offered for the dead as well.
** Here St. Augustine testifies not only to the belief in prayers for the dead (i.e., an implicit acknowledgement of Purgatory), he also bears witness to the intercession of Saints in heaven.

# Appendix B

# *Old Testament Canon of Scripture*

One of the misunderstandings that I frequently hear regarding the Catholic Church is that she "added" to the Scriptures seven Old Testament writings that are not found in Protestant Bibles. These books are: *Tobit, Judith, The Wisdom of Solomon (Wisdom), Sirach (Ecclesiasticus), Baruch, 1 Maccabees, and 2 Maccabees.*

It is commonly asserted by Protestant apologists that the books in question were added to the Catholic Bible at the sixteenth century Council of Trent in response to Protestantism. For example, Norman L. Geisler and William E. Nix, two prominent Protestant biblical scholars, state the following:

> The Council of Trent (1545-63) was the first official proclamation of the Roman Catholic Church on the Apocrypha, and it came a millennium and a half after the books were written, in an obvious polemical action against Protestantism. Furthermore, the addition of books that support salvation by works and prayers for the dead at that time—only twenty-nine years after Luther posted his Ninety-five Theses—is highly suspect.[48]

This assertion is intended to imply that the Catholic Church added these books in a shameless attempt to bolster her doctrinal positions on prayers for the dead and the role of good works in salvation. This simply does not square, however, with the facts of history.

Did the Council of Trent solemnly define the canon of Scripture used by Catholics even to this day? Yes, it did. But in doing so, she did *not* add a single "jot" or "tittle" to Catholic Bibles. The fact is that the Catholic Church has utilized the same Old Testament canon of Scripture *from the beginning*. Consider, if you will, the following historical facts:

1. The version of the Old Testament Scriptures most often quoted and utilized by Christ and the apostles was the Septuagint (LXX), a Greek translation of the Hebrew Scriptures, which originated in Alexandria, Egypt, in the third century B.C. The Septuagint utilized the Alexandrian Canon, which included the books that Protestants dispute. This fact is testified to by ancient collections of Sacred Scripture. These collections (or codices) include the *Codex Vaticanus* (fourth century A.D.), the *Codex Sinaiticus* (fourth century A.D.), and the *Codex Alexandrinus* (fifth century A.D.). All three of these ancient manuscripts bear testimony to the acceptance of the disputed books by the earliest Christians.

2. The early Fathers of the Church unhesitatingly quoted from these books, thereby demonstrating the early Church's acceptance of these books. Consider the following examples:

"You shall not waver with regard to your decisions (Sirach 1:28). Do not be someone who stretches out his hands to receive but withdraws when it comes to giving" (Sirach 4:31, quoted in the *Didache*, 4:5, circa A.D. 70-160).

"By the word of His might (God) established all things, and by His word He can overthrow them. 'Who shall say to Him, "What have you done?" or who shall resist the power of His strength?'" (Wisdom 12:12, quoted in the *Epistle to the Corinthians*, St. Clement of Rome, circa A.D. 80).

When you can do good, defer it not, because 'alms deliver from death'" (Tobit 4:10 and 12:9, quoted in the *Epistle to the Philadephians,* 10, St. Polycarp, circa. A.D. 135).

3. Ancient Church councils and papal decrees defined and reiterated the list of sacred books, which agrees with Catholic Bibles today:

a. A.D. 382: Pope Damasus convoked a synod that produced the Roman Code. The Roman Code identified a list of Holy Scripture identical to the Council of Trent's formally defined canon.

b. A.D. 393: The Council of Hippo (a regional council of Catholic bishops) produced a list of canonical Scripture identical to that formally defined by the Council of Trent.

c. A.D. 397: First Council of Carthage (another regional council of Catholic bishops) produced a list of canonical Scripture identical to that formally defined by the Council of Trent.

d. A.D. 405: Pope Innocent I wrote a letter to the Gallican bishop Exsuperius of Toulouse that listed the books of Scripture (again, a list that conforms perfectly to that defined at Trent).

e. A.D. 419: Second Council of Carthage.

4. The first printed Bible was produced by Johannes Gutenberg in Mainz, Germany, between 1450 and 1456. Like *all* Bibles of its day, the Gutenberg Bible contained the longer canon of Old Testament Scriptures, and therefore was identical to the Catholic Bible of today.[49]

So while non-Catholics are free to argue against the inclusion of the disputed books in the canon of Scripture, they cannot maintain any semblance of integrity if, in the course of such argumentation, they erroneously assert that the Catholic Church added those books at the Council of Trent. The facts of history clearly refute such a claim.

For 1,500 years prior to the Council of Trent, Catholics utilized the longer canon of Old Testament Scripture. Approximately 100 years before Trent, the Council of Florence (1431-1437) affirmed the same canon of Scripture. Why, then, did the Church feel the need to solemnly define the canon of Scripture at Trent? Precisely because certain Protestant leaders were recklessly mutilating the Bible by removing from the canon of Holy Writ that which it had included from the beginning. Therefore, the real question is this: *By what authority did the Protestant Reformers remove these seven books from the Bible?* Ironically, Protestants often scoff at the Catholic Church's claim to infallibility. Yet, by presuming to *remove* seven books from the Bible, were not the early Protestant Reformers, in effect, assuming for themselves the charism of infallibility?

## Appendix C

# *Eucharistic Prayer II*

Excerpts from Eucharistic Prayer II from the Sacramentary of the Roman Missal are provided below for the purpose of comparing it to the Eucharistic prayers recorded for us by St. Hippolytus of Rome in A.D. 215 and cited in Chapter 15, *Christ in the Fullness of Worship.* Such a comparison suffices to demonstrate that the modern Catholic liturgy is not a mutation that occurred over several centuries but is organically identical to the worship of the earliest recorded Christian liturgies.

### Eucharistic Prayer II

Priest:   The Lord be with you.
People:  And also with you.

Priest:   Lift up your hearts.
People:  We lift them up to the Lord.

Priest:   Let us give thanks to the Lord.
People:  It is right to give Him thanks and praise.

Priest: Father, it is our duty and salvation, always and everywhere to give You thanks through Your beloved Son, Jesus Christ. He is the Word through whom You made the universe, the Savior

You sent to redeem us. By the power of the Holy Spirit he took flesh and was born of the Virgin Mary. For our sake He opened his arms on the cross; He put an end to death and revealed the resurrection. In this He fulfilled your will and won for you a Holy people...Before He was given up to death, a death he freely accepted, he took bread and gave thanks. He broke the bread, gave it to His disciples, and said: "Take this, all of you, and eat it: This is My body which will be given up for you." When supper was ended, He took the cup. Again He gave you thanks and praise, gave the cup to His disciples, and said: "Take this, all of you, and drink from it: This is the cup of My blood, the blood of the new and everlasting covenant. It will be shed for you and for all so that sins may be forgiven. Do this in memory of Me."

Priest:  In memory of His death and resurrection, we offer You, Father, this life-giving bread, this saving cup. We thank You for counting us worthy to stand in Your presence and serve You. May all of us who share in the body and blood of Christ be brought together in unity by the Holy Spirit...

## Appendix D

# *Scandals Must Come*

It is very disconcerting for inquirers to the Catholic faith to encounter lifelong Catholics who nonchalantly dismiss crucial Church teachings concerning faith and morals. Yet, sadly, it is not an uncommon occurrence. After one such encounter with a *priest*, I went home feeling nearly demoralized. I can remember wondering if I had been bamboozled into searching for something that actually did not exist. It made me angry. I felt like throwing in the towel.

When I awoke the next morning, however, the questions that had initially pointed me towards Rome continued to haunt me. They *demanded* answers, and the answers were all coming from the direction of the Catholic Church. Yet, I sometimes found myself in danger of allowing the presence of scandals in the Church to overshadow and even obscure the beauty of the truths that she was holding out to me. For this reason, it may prove helpful for some to take a look at scandals in the Church in the light of Scripture.

Go back with me about 2,000 years, to the city of Corinth. There you would find a group of Christians whom St. Paul identified as "the church of God which is at Corinth" who were "called to be saints" (1 Corinthians 1:2). So far, so good. Later, however, St. Paul upbraided this same church for tolerating among themselves sins that not even the pagans would endure. That is quite a statement, considering what pagans were doing in first-century Corinth. The point, however, is: If someone had written off the Church because of the scandal amongst the Christians of Corinth, he would have stumbled off the path, failing to follow the example of St. Paul himself who never gave up on them.

Consider also the seven churches of Asia Minor addressed by our Lord in the opening chapters of the Book of Revelation. The majority of them were rebuked, not commended:

> To the Church at Ephesus, our Lord said, "I have this against you, that you have abandoned the love you had at first" (Revelation 2:4).

> To the Church at Pergamum, our Lord said, "You have some there who hold to the teaching of Balaam, who taught Balak to put a stumbling block before the sons of Israel, that they might eat food sacrificed to idols and practice immorality" (Revelation 2:14).

> To the Church at Thyatira, our Lord said, "I have this against you, that you tolerate the woman Jezebel, who calls herself a prophetess and is teaching and beguiling my servants to practice immorality" (Revelation 2:20).

> To the Church at Sardis, our Lord said, "You have the name of being alive, and you are dead" (Revelation 3:1).

> Finally, to the Church at Laodicea, Jesus said, "I know your works: You are neither cold nor hot. Would that you were cold or hot! So, because you are lukewarm, and neither cold nor hot, I will spew you out of My mouth. For you say, I am rich, I have prospered, and I need nothing; not knowing that you are wretched, pitiable, poor, blind and naked" (Revelation 3:15-17).

Remember, these statements were all addressed by our Lord to *His Church!*

Now, that is not to make light of immorality, heresy, or lukewarmness. It is, rather, to simply underscore the fact that, *from the beginning,* the Church of God has comprised less-than-perfect people—people who could and did cause scandal.

Recall also the parable of the wheat and the tares (Matthew 13:24-30). There we find Jesus likening the Kingdom of God to a field in which had been sown both wheat and tares (weeds). Our Lord said that both were to remain until the final harvest (the Last Day) at which time "the Son of man will send His angels, and they will gather out of His kingdom all causes of sin and all evildoers, and throw them into the furnace of fire" (Matthew 13:41-42).

Finally, consider the most profound words of our Lord concerning scandals. He said, "Temptations to sin are sure to come; but woe to him by whom they come" (Luke 17:2). The phrase translated "temptations to sin" is literally "scandals" in the original Greek text. In other words, Jesus is saying, "Scandals are sure to come." But why are they "sure to come"? Why is it "impossible" that they should not come?* That which is "sure" to happen or "impossible" to avoid must, of necessity, be permitted by God. Moreover, it is axiomatic that God permits nothing that cannot be used by Him for our good and to bring greater glory to His name. So, *why* does the Lord who loves us so permit scandals? One possible reason is to help each of us grow in *humility*.

It is so easy to pass judgment upon others. It is so easy to forget that the Church is a community of believers comprising both the weak and the strong, the immature and the mature. The weak and the immature may very well fall into sins that cause scandal. In such instances, those who consider themselves to be "strong" and "mature" in their faith can find themselves looking down their noses at the weak with pharisaical indignation. God's will, however, is that those who are strong should bear the burdens of the weak. In so doing, we demonstrate the charity of Christ, who chose not to despise us for our weaknesses but to become one with us that we might share in His life. For us to imitate Christ in this way requires that we face the truth about

---

* The King James Version states, "It is impossible but that offenses will come."

ourselves and the truth about others...and that requires humility. And as long as we all stand in need of humility, "scandals are sure to come."

# *The Mode of Baptism*

To speak of the mode of baptism is to speak of the specific action employed in the sacrament, whether pouring, sprinkling, or immersion. Both as a Southern Baptist and as a member of the Stone-Campbell Churches of Christ, I had been taught that the *only* acceptable mode for Baptism is immersion (and more to the point, total submersion). I was even under the impression that those who baptized by other modes, such as pouring or sprinkling, *knew* that the Bible did not support their position but loved their own traditions so much that they preferred them to the Word of God. It was not until I began to study the Catholic faith that I learned differently.

The controversy revolves, in large part, around the definition of the Greek word *baptizo,* the word from which the English word *baptism* is derived. The following brief study is intended to highlight some of the philological, scriptural, and historical facts pertinent to the word *baptizo* as it is used in reference to the sacrament of baptism and, thereby, demonstrate that Baptism by modes *other* than complete submersion have been acceptable from the earliest days of the Church. The scope of this book does not allow for an exhaustive treatment of the subject. What is offered here, therefore, is intended to simply whet the appetite of those specific readers who choose to study the matter further.

## *Baptizo* in Classic Greek

Most often, Christians who are strict immersionists take the track that all "reputable" lexicographers and scholars agree with the immersionist's understanding of the meaning of *baptizo*. They often assert that it is nonsensical to speak of the *mode* of the word *baptizo* for, according to them, the word speaks of mode and mode only. Being a former immersionist, I can well remember believing—and teaching—that if the word *baptizo* was accurately translated in our English Bibles, they would have the word "immersion" in the place of "baptism" whenever the Greek word *baptizo* is used. This oversimplification, however, is not supported by philological studies, history, or the Scriptures.

For example, when referenced to physical mode, *baptizo* does *not* usually indicate the act of dipping characteristic of baptism as practiced by immersionists. In a study of 175 uses of *baptizo* in ancient Greek writings, Dr. T.J. Conant (a Baptist) translated *baptizo* with some form of the English word *dip* only ten times.[50] The following quotes from Dr. Conant's study illustrate the point:

> *"Polybius, History, book VIII, ch. 8,4.* Describing the operations of the engines, which Archimedes constructed for the defense of Syracuse when besieged by the Romans, and with which he lifted the prows of the besieging vessels out of the water, so that they stood erect on the stern, and then let them fall, he says: *'Which being done, some of the vessels fell on their side, and some were overturned; but most of them, when the prow was let fall from on high, BEING SUBMERGED (BAPTIZED), became filled with sea-water and confusion.'"* [51]

> *"Didorus (the Sicilian), Historical Library, book XVI. ch. 80.* In his account of Timoleon's defeat of the Carthaginian army on the bank of the river Crimissus in Sicily, many of the fugitives perishing in the stream swollen by a violent storm, he says:

'The river, rushing down with the current increased in violence,
SUBMERGED (BAPTIZED) many, and destroyed them attempting
to swim through their armour.'" [52]

"Diodorus (the Sicilian), Historical Library, book I, ch. 36.
Describing the effects of the rapid rise of the water during
the annual inundation of the Nile, he says: 'Most of the wild
land animals are surrounded by the stream and perish, being
SUBMERGED (BAPTIZED); but some, escaping to the high
grounds, are saved.'"[53]

This is significant because, as stated earlier, the case made
by immersionists rests primarily upon the "fact" that the classical
definition of *baptizo* dictates their mode of dipping. Thus they
baptize by placing one completely under the water followed by
immediate removal from the water. However, it seems that more
often than not, *baptizo* indicates an immersion *without* dipping. In
other words, the word translated "baptism" in the New Testament
Scriptures, when indicating submersion or immersion, does not
indicate the subsequent re-emergence of the subject from the fluid
in that it does not usually indicate dipping but something more akin
to drowning. Moreover, the Greek word that *does* signify the act
of dipping or placing an object under a fluid followed by removal
from the fluid is the word *bapto*. While *bapto* is a cognate of
*baptizo*, it is not the word that is translated "baptism" or "baptize"
in the Sacred Scriptures. In fact, *bapto* quite often signifies dipping
but *without* complete submersion as the following examples from
the *Septuagint** and the New Testament Scriptures demonstrate.

And you shall take a bunch of hyssop, dip (LXX: bapto; Hebrew:
tabal) it in the blood that is in the basin, and strike the lintel and the
two doorposts with the blood that is in the basin (Exodus 12:22).

* The Septuagint (LXX) was the Greek translation of the Old Testament Scriptures
which scholars—both Catholic and Protestant—agree was the text most often
quoted by Jesus and the Apostles. It is extremely valuable for showing how the Jews
employed the Greek Language.

> As for the living bird, he shall take it, the cedar wood and the scarlet and the hyssop, and dip (LXX: *bapto*; Hebrew: *tabal*) them and the living bird in the blood of the bird that was killed over the running water (Leviticus 14:6).

> Then the priest shall dip (LXX: *bapto*; Hebrew: *tabal*) his right finger in the oil that is in his left hand (Leviticus 14:16).

> A clean person shall take hyssop and dip (LXX: *bapto*; Hebrew: *tabal*) it in the water, sprinkle it on the tent, on all the vessels, on the persons who were there, or on the one who touched a bone, the slain, the dead, or a grave (Numbers 19:18).

> Now Boaz said to her at mealtime, 'Come here, and eat of the bread, and dip (LXX: *bapto*; Hebrew: *tabal*) your piece of bread in the vinegar (Ruth 2:14).

> Jesus answered, 'It is he to whom I shall give a piece of bread when I have dipped (*bapto*) it (John 13:26).

In other words, *baptizo* (the word translated "baptism" in the New Testament Scriptures), while often signifying immersion, does not usually signify a dipping action, whereas *bapto* (the word most often translated "dip") often indicates dipping without complete submersion. Therefore, even when physical action is involved in relation to a fluid, *baptizo*, in classical Greek literature, does not usually correspond to the action of baptism by immersion as practiced by modern Christian immersionists.

Finally, *baptizo* is quite often used to refer not to a physical action at all but to an effect or the agency of effect, as the following examples demonstrate (*baptizo* here is translated as "mersed"):

> But he, **mersed** by anger, is subdued; and wishing to escape into his own domain is no longer free, but is forced to hate the object loved (*Achilles Tatius*). [54]

The drink which **merses**...(*Seneca*).[55]

On account of the abundant revenue from these sources, they do not **merse** the people with taxes" (*Diodorus Siculus*).[56]

(He was) great at Salamis; for there, fighting, he **mersed** all Asia (*Heimerius*).[57]

But when he does not so continue, being **mersed** by diseases and by arts of wizards..." (*Plotinus*).[58]

**Mersed** by worldly affairs—we should struggle out and try to save ourselves, and reach the harbor" (*Plutarch*).[59]

After nearly 350 pages of detailed analysis of citations from classical Greek writings, Presbyterian scholar John W. Dale, drew the logical conclusion:

Whatever is capable of thoroughly changing the character, state, or condition of any object, is capable of baptizing that object; and by such change of character, state, or condition does, in fact, baptize it." [60]

Such is the use of *baptizo* in classical Greek literature. Now let us consider how the word is employed in Sacred Scripture.

## *Baptizo* in Sacred Scripture

Immersionists often set up a straw man by arguing that the word *baptizo* and its cognates never mean "pour" or "sprinkle." Yet, Catholics and other Christians who baptize by pouring (infusion) or sprinkling (aspersion) never have argued that the word *baptizo* literally means "pour" or "sprinkle." That is *not* the question. The question is: How is the word *baptizo* used in the Bible? We have already seen that in classical Greek usage, *baptizo* can—but does not necessarily—indicate submersion. Now what must be considered is its usage in Scripture.

There is no end to the number of examples that can be provided of words taking on connotations that are not identical with their original, literal meanings. Take, for example, the word "canon" (from the Greek *kanon*). The word originally indicated a physical object, specifically a measuring rod. Through development and usage, however, it came to signify one's sphere of activity or limits of authority (e.g., 2 Corinthians 10:13, 15) and, metaphorically, any rule of living or standard as such (e.g., Galatians 6:16 and Philippians 3:16). By extension, canon came also to be used in referring to an authoritative list as in the case of the canon of Scripture. By the same token, *baptizo* has undergone development in terms of its meaning and associated nuances. As the following citations from Scripture demonstrate, the Jews had come to use the word *baptizo* to refer to ceremonial washings and purification rites in general, washings that most often did *not* involve the physical mode of submersion but of pouring and sprinkling. In other words, both the Greek translation of the Old Testament (the Septuagint) and the Greek text of the New Testament use the word *baptizo* in ways that simply do not fit a rigid approach that limits the word to literal submersion.

> According to this arrangement, gifts and sacrifices are offered which cannot perfect the conscience of the worshiper, but deal only with food and drink and various ablutions, regulations for the body imposed until the time of reformation (Hebrews 9:10).

The word translated "ablutions" is a plural cognate of *baptizo*. The context clearly indicates that the ablutions being referred to are the various ceremonial washings of the Old Testament. Yet, as we look at those ablutions, we do not see submersions *per se* (at least not of the kind that Christian immersionists advocate). For example, Leviticus 15:5 gives instructions concerning purification for those made unclean through contact with a man who has a "discharge." The instructions call for those who are unclean to simply "bathe." The Greek word employed in the Septuagint translation is *baptizo*.

In the verses immediately following the above text from Hebrews, it is clear that the "ablutions" being referred to include purification rites involving sprinkling. Hebrews 9:11-14, for example, refers to "the sprinkling of defiled persons with the blood of goats and bulls and the ashes of a heifer." The background for this purification rite is found in Numbers 19:1-22. Therefore, what we see here is that the word "baptism" was being used to refer to purification rites and washings in general. These purifications of the Mosaic Law (e.g., Leviticus 14:4-7, Psalm 51:2, 7, *et. al.*) were seen by the Fathers of the Church as foreshadowings or types of Christian Baptism. They varied in terms of their physical modes, but their effect was the same: *cleansing.*[61]

> And when they come from the marketplace, they do not eat unless they purify themselves (Mark 7:4).

The word translated "purify" is *baptizo*.[62] The text actually states that, after visiting the marketplace, the Jews refused to eat unless they first "baptized themselves." Does this mean that whenever they went shopping they came home and literally submerged their entire bodies in water before eating? No. In fact, Mark 7:2 reveals that the context of this statement was a controversy concerning the washing of *hands*. While it could well be that in washing their hands the Jews submerged or dipped their hands in water, verse 4 indicates that in so doing they were said to have "baptized themselves." While only the hands were immersed, the entire person was said to have been "baptized" because the word *baptizo* was used by the Jews to refer to ceremonial purifications in general.

> The Pharisee was astonished to see that He did not first wash before dinner (Luke 11:38).

In all three major Greek texts (the Textus Receptus, the Westcott-Hort, and the Byzantine Majority), the word translated "wash" is a cognate of *baptizo*. As in Mark 7:4, *baptizo* is used by the sacred writer simply to refer to ceremonial purification by means of washing (without any implicit reference to mode *per se*).

## *Baptizo* and the Sacrament of Baptism

As we have seen, *baptizo* is a highly nuanced word that cannot be presumed to indicate a literal, physical submersion. Rather, the word was used by the Jews and the inspired writers of the Scriptures to refer to ceremonial washings in a more general sense, regardless of physical mode. Therefore, when we arrive at the subject of the proper mode for the Sacrament of baptism, we should not be surprised to find that the Scriptures do not explicitly prescribe a particular mode. In fact, while the Scriptures command us to baptize and provide us with several descriptions of the *effects* of baptism, they do not provide any instructions as to *how* to actually baptize.

Immersionists would counter this by citing the Baptism of the Ethiopian eunuch as a Scriptural example of how to baptize. We read:

> And they both went down into the water, Philip and the eunuch, and he baptized him. And when they came up out of the water, the Spirit of the Lord caught up Philip; and the eunuch saw him no more, and went on his way rejoicing" (Acts 8:38-39).

Immersionists focus on the words, "they went down...he baptized him...they came up." The going down and coming up, however, do not indicate Baptism by submersion because *both* Philip and the eunuch "went down" and "came up." In other words, the picture is one of both Philip and the Ethiopian going down (from the chariot) to a pool of water (of unspecified depth) for the purpose of baptizing the eunuch. The mode of baptism, therefore, is not specified. In pointing to this example immersionists are begging the question as to what is meant by the word "baptized."

The earliest written instruction that we have on how to actually baptize is found in the first century document called the *Didache*. Also known as the *Teaching of the Twelve Apostles*, this document composed between A.D. 70 and A.D. 100 is a short treatise that was highly regarded by the early Church. In chapter seven, we read:

> And concerning baptism, baptize this way: Having first said all these things, baptize into the name of the Father, and of the Son, and of the Holy Spirit, in living water. But if you have no living water, baptize into other water; and if you cannot do so in cold water, do so in warm. But if you have neither, pour out water three times upon the head into the name of Father and Son and Holy Spirit.

Here we find solid evidence that the early Church regarded baptism by pouring to be acceptable (which also fits what we have seen regarding the usage of the word *baptizo* in Scripture). Moreover, whether by immersion or by pouring, early Christian baptism—according to the historical testimony of the *Didache*—involved either a *triple* immersion or a *triple* pouring (which is, still to this day, the practice of the Catholic Church).*

---

* "Baptism is performed in the most expressive way by triple immersion in the baptismal water. However, from ancient times it has also been able to be conferred by pouring water three times over the candidate's head" (*CCC*, No. 1239).

Finally, the archaeological evidence overwhelmingly indicates that the early Church accepted baptism by either pouring or a form of immersion that did not involve total submersion (in which case "immersion" is to be loosely understood as referring to a thorough washing or wetting, as indicated by the classical and scriptural examples already considered). This evidence takes the form of artistic depiction and the design of baptismal fonts or pools. In this regard, consider the following.

> Nearly 400 examples of ecclesiastical fonts belonging to the period 230-680 A.D. have been located...Only a very few of the early fonts could have been used for total immersion even supposing they were filled to capacity. Most depths range from about 35 cm (14 inches) to a little over a meter (40 inches), but typically 60 cm (2 feet), half the depth commonly considered necessary for immersionists today.[63]

> The fonts discovered show that the general practice was for the candidate to enter the bath by (usually) two steps, and stand in water up to his ankles, knees, or loins. His head was then dipped in a basin arrangement called the laver, or else the water was simply poured. Drawings on the walls of the catacombs and elsewhere back into the second century show a similar mode.[64]

Do modern Protestant Christians who baptize by immersion follow the practice of the early Church and use a triple immersion? No, they do not. When I once asked an immersionist preacher about this he dismissed the point as being nothing more than a cavil (a false or frivolous objection). However, the point is not a frivolous one, for it points to a very serious issue: namely, *authority*. In view of the fact that the word *baptizo* (as employed by the Jews and the sacred writers) does not—of itself—prescribe a particular mode of washing, and in view of the fact that the Scriptures do not provide any explicit instructions on *how* to baptize, how do modern "Bible *only*" Christians know that they are baptizing properly?

The point I am making is simply this: Baptism, like all matters pertaining to the practice of the Christian faith, boils down to *authority*. As Chapter 12 of this book demonstrates, the "Bible *only*" approach to authority is deeply flawed, unworkable, and, in the final analysis, decidedly unscriptural. The Scriptures themselves point to the Church as "the pillar and support of the truth" (1 Timothy 3:15). In regard to baptism, the constant teaching and practice of the Church *from the beginning* has been to recognize *both* immersion and pouring as valid modes for the sacrament. While immersionists, therefore, sincerely believe that they are standing solidly upon the Word of God, the practice of recognizing *only* those baptisms that are performed by total submersion is, in the final analysis, a *tradition of men* and completely foreign to the apostolic Deposit of Faith.

## Appendix F

# *"Call No Man Father"*

In the twenty-third chapter of Matthew's Gospel, we have the well-known discourse of our Lord in which He upbraided the scribes and the Pharisees for their flagrant hypocrisy. Jesus began His rebuke of the scribes and Pharisees by describing their love for human respect:

> Then spake Jesus to the multitude, and to his disciples, saying, "The scribes and the Pharisees sit in Moses' seat: All therefore whatsoever they bid you observe, that observe and do; but do not ye after their works: for they say and do not. For they bind heavy burdens and grievous to be borne, and lay them on men's shoulders; but they themselves will not move them with one of their fingers. But all their works they do for to be seen of men: They make broad their phylacteries, and enlarge the borders of their garments, and love the uppermost rooms at feasts, and the chief seats in the synagogues, and greetings in the markets, and to be called of men, Rabbi, Rabbi. But be not ye called Rabbi: for one is your Master, even Christ; and all ye are brethren. And call no man your father upon the earth: for one is your Father, which is in heaven. Neither be ye called masters: for one is your Master, even Christ. But he that is greatest among you shall be your servant. And whoever shall exalt himself shall be abased; and he that shall humble himself shall be exalted" (Matthew 23:1-12).[*]

As a former fundamentalist, I am well aware of the concern created in the minds of non-Catholic Christians when, in verse

---

[*] All Scriptural citations in Appendix F are from the Authorized King James Version.

nine, they see our Lord telling the Jews to "call no man your father upon the earth." For many non-Catholic Christians, this admonition of Christ constitutes a "proof" against the legitimacy of the Catholic faith because Catholics refer to their priests as "father."

Yet, it is obvious that this critique is driven by anti-Catholic bias because I've never heard the same critics emphasizing the rest of what Jesus said in the immediate context: "be not ye called Rabbi" (teacher) or "neither be ye called masters" (Mr. = mister = master).

But what did our Lord *mean* when He said, "Call no man your father upon earth"? We know what He *said*, but what did He *mean*? At this point, I am sure many will do as I once did and exclaim, "Well, He meant what He said, and He said what He meant!" Such an simplified approach overlooks the fact that there were times when our blessed Lord said things that were *not* meant to be taken literally or at mere face value.

For example, our Lord's instructions to pluck out an eye or cut off a hand that makes one stumble (Matthew 5:29-30). No Christian today would say that a man struggling with the lust of the flesh should gouge his eyes out. For one thing, lust, like all sins being a matter of the heart, would not be cured by merely losing one's physical sense of sight. Likewise, the thief who cuts off his hand will not thereby uproot the covetousness in his heart. Our Lord used strong and graphic words, words He did not intend to be followed in a literal sense, to convey a deep and fundamental truth—namely, that we should allow nothing to stand between us and our soul's salvation. The question is, was this particular warning from Jesus one of those instances?

The fact that our Lord did not mean for us to understand these words in the strict, literal sense can be seen by the way in which the word "father" is used throughout the Scriptures. *Father* occurs hundreds of times in the Scriptures, but consider the following sampling:

1. St. Stephen's words to the Jewish Sanhedrin: "Men, brethren, and *fathers*, hearken; The God of glory appeared unto our father Abraham, when he was in Mesopotamia, before he dwelt in Haran" (Acts 7:2).

2. St. Paul's Letter to the Romans: "Therefore it is of faith, that it might be by grace; to the end the promise might be sure to all the seed; not to that only which is of the law, but to that also which is of the faith of Abraham, who is the *father* of us all" (Romans 4:16).

3. St. Paul's words to the Jews at Jerusalem (Acts 22:1): "Men, brethren, and *fathers*, hear ye my defense which I make now unto you" (Acts 22:1).

4. St. Paul's words to the Corinthians (where he makes no bones about it, he is the spiritual father of the Corinthians and refers to them as his children, as he does Timothy, Titus, and Onesimus): "I write not these things to shame you, but as my beloved sons I warn you. For though ye have ten thousand instructors in Christ, yet have ye not many *fathers:* for in Christ Jesus I have begotten you through the gospel" (I Corinthians 4:14-15).

These are simply four examples out of hundreds that refer to men as fathers. Please note that these verses demonstrate the propriety of referring to certain individuals as "father" even in a spiritual sense. This being the case, what *did* our Lord mean when He said, "Call no man your father upon earth"?

The answer is found in the context of our Lord's statement. This reveals that He was addressing the obsession that the scribes and Pharisees had with human respect. Verse twelve makes it clear that our Lord's point was to call men to humility.

Humility, as St. Teresa of Avila tells us, is *the truth*. Humility is the truth about ourselves, the truth about others, and the truth about God. Regarding the subject presently under discussion, humility is the truth about fatherhood as well. *That* truth—the truth about fatherhood—is stated by Jesus in verse nine and reiterated by St. Paul in his letter to the Ephesians 3:14-15:

> "For this cause I bow my knees to the Father of our Lord Jesus
> Christ, of whom all paternity in heaven and earth is named."*

That truth is simply that *all fatherhood is rooted in God the
Father*. Fatherhood, be it spiritual or physical, is pleasing in
God's sight when it is humbly exercised in His name.

Catholic priests, in begetting and nourishing spiritual children
through the Gospel and the sacraments are, in the *deepest* sense
of the word, truly fathers. Therefore, it is entirely appropriate
that they be referred to as such. To attempt to employ our Lord's
words in Matthew 23:9 against this practice is only possible if
one ignores the rest of Scripture and the practice of the Apostles
and the early Church.

---

* Some translations say "family." The original Greek, however, is literally translated
"*paternity*" (fatherhood). In other words, all fatherhood is derived from God *the*
Father.

# Appendix G

# *Do Doctrines Develop?*

It is common knowledge that the Catholic Church believes in the development of doctrine. However, this concept can be difficult for many non-Catholics, especially if one has a fundamentalist or conservative Evangelical background. I can well remember one of my former teachers scoffing at the concept and vehemently stating, "Doctrines don't develop!" Within his own "restorationist" tradition, however, doctrines have been developing ever since Campbell, Stone, and others launched the movement.

Most Church of Christ apologists, nonetheless, insist that doctrines don't develop; only our understanding of them. They approach the New Testament as they would a blueprint seeking to discover, by study over time, the details of the "pattern" and how to implement them. They believe that the Lord delivered this pattern to the Church and that men must study and reflect upon it for the purpose of understanding and implementing it. They also recognize, however, that individuals and, hence the Church, can grow in the knowledge of this pattern. If this were not so, Churches of Christ would not have a history of splintering and splitting, which happens quite often whenever someone discovers a "new" aspect of the "pattern" or claims a new insight into already known details. This is essentially how the Churches of Christ have gotten to where they are today, following their own version of the "development of doctrine."

The Catholic Church's understanding of the development of doctrine is similar but crucially different. The Catholic Church teaches that the apostles, handing on what they themselves had received, warn the faithful to hold fast to the traditions which they have learned either by word or mouth or by letter (cf. Thessalonians 2:15)."[65] In addition, this "Tradition which comes from the apostles develops in the Church with the help of the Holy Spirit."[66] Thus, from the seed first planted by Christ and passed through the Apostles, grows the mustard tree that is the Church. For through this natural, Spirit led development, that which is implicit becomes more and more explicit.

Fundamentally the same in principle, the Stone-Campbell Churches of Christ version of the development of doctrine and the Catholic version, therefore, have at least one crucial difference: For the Churches of Christ, the development of doctrine often entails the addition of something completely new and previously unknown to the brotherhood; the Catholic understanding, on the other hand, does not.

In the Churches of Christ, many "discoveries" by brethren over the years have introduced new concepts completely at odds with prior practice and belief, which is why splinters and splits result. In the Catholic Church, developments and definitions have always been the natural outworking and application of what the Church has already believed. It has never amounted to "pulling a rabbit out of the hat;" a new dogmatic definition is never something that was previously foreign to the practice of the Catholic faith.

Take any Catholic doctrine you like: the primacy of the Petrine office, the Real Presence of Christ in the Eucharist, the hypostatic union (the two natures of Christ united in one Person), or the Marian doctrines. None of these materialized out of thin air; rather, each expresses a clarification over time, through the Church's continued reflection and contemplation, under the guidance of the Holy Spirit, of truth that can be traced back (either explicitly or implicitly) to Sacred Scripture and the Apostolic Deposit of Faith.

It's important to recognize that every explicit teaching of Scripture carries with it implicit or hidden corollaries. These become apparent over time as the explicit teachings confront new situations, issues, or sometimes novel, erroneous interpretations. Sometimes this time frame is short, other times it is extensive, but the process is never completely exhausted because the Deposit of Faith pertains to mysteries that exceed mere human comprehension. Therefore, as time rolls on and the Church continues to reflect upon the Deposit of Faith (each generation standing on the shoulders of the previous generation), doctrinal development continues because the implications of that which has been "once for all delivered to the saints" continue to unfold for us.

So when we look at any particular doctrine of the faith, we can see its development over time. For example, the teaching that Christ has two wills, one human and the other divine. That was an implication derived from an explicit teaching of Scripture. The explicit teaching is that "the Word became flesh and dwelt among us" (John 1:14). The implications of this explicit teaching, however, are inexhaustible. One of these implications is that Christ—to be fully God and fully man—must have had two wills. This implication was not drawn out, made explicit, and defined until the Monothelite heresy arose in the seventh century. Over the centuries, many views, each carrying its own set of further and often contradictory implications, had arisen on this issue. In response, the bishops of the Church, who had gathered at the Council of Constantinople, after prayerfully examining the variety of views, ruled definitively that Christ had two wills (one human, the other divine). Was this ruling an innovation? No. It was an example of Christ fulfilling His promise that the Holy Spirit would guide His Church into all the truth by helping her discern which of the many conflicting views was true.

Moreover, recognizing this work of the Holy Spirit in the development of doctrine, a formerly implicit truth that is made explicit by the teaching authority of the Church ("the pillar and support of the truth") becomes binding upon the consciences of the faithful. As Jesus told His Apostles, "He who hears you, hears Me" (Luke 10:16). So, when we consider the previous example of the two wills of Christ, we see that prior to the seventh century, the Church had made no explicit decision on this matter. Consequently, there were no anathemas attached to anyone who had denied this dogma. Nonetheless, this teaching had been present all along, implicit in the explicit teachings on the Incarnation in the Deposit of Faith.

By way of imperfect illustration, consider the relationship of parent to child. The child, at the earliest age possible, is given a "Deposit of Faith." This deposit contains basically one explicitly stated dogma: "Obey your parents!" This one explicit teaching, however, has an endless number of implicit corollaries, which are unfolded and made explicit as the child matures. At the age of two this may involve simply staying away from stove heating units and electrical outlets, while at the age of seventeen it may include directives concerning evening curfews. Each implicit corollary that becomes explicitly defined over time was contained, however, in the initial, explicit deposit: "Obey your parents!" In this sense, the child's understanding of truth undergoes development.

In reality, it could be said that from the beginning the Church had always embraced the teaching that there were two wills in Christ. This she had done only implicitly by embracing the entire Deposit of Faith and all its implications, knowing that some of these implications would only become clear in the future.

Finally, it should be noted that this process of doctrinal development is modeled for us in Sacred Scripture. Recall that on the day of Pentecost, St. Peter, citing the prophet Joel, said, "In the last days it shall be, God declares, that I will pour out my Spirit upon all flesh" (Acts 1:17). He then told his hearers, "The promise is to you and to your children and to all that are far off, every one whom the Lord our God calls to Him" (Acts 2:39). In other words, the Deposit of Faith, as given to Peter and preached by him, implicitly included the Gentiles (that is, "all flesh" and "those who are far off"). Peter, however, did not grasp that truth until years later when he received the vision of the sheet being let down from Heaven (Acts 10:9-23). It was then that he went to the house of the Roman centurion, Cornelius, and declared, "Truly I perceive that God shows no partiality, but in every nation any one who fears Him and does what is right is acceptable to Him" (Acts 10:34-35). This insight was subsequently related to the entire Church at the Council of Jerusalem (Acts 15:1-29) where what was formerly implicit was made explicit.

By this example, the Scriptures bear witness to the Holy Spirit guiding the apostolic leadership in the process of the development in doctrine—a process that will continue as long as time endures.

## Appendix H

# *Peter and the Papacy*

Protestant Christians are often under the impression that the papacy has no foundation in Scripture. It is often asserted by anti-Catholic apologists that the papacy did not exist until centuries after the Church was established. As the patristic citations in Appendix A demonstrate, however, the Church has always acknowledged the primacy of St. Peter and his successors, the Bishops of Rome. Moreover, this primacy is rooted firmly in the teachings of Sacred Scripture.

The following study outline is offered as a primer for further, individual study of the papacy. For an in depth treatment of this subject, I highly recommend two books: *Jesus, Peter & the Keys*[67] and *Upon This Rock*.[69] In addition, serious inquirers may want to read Patrick Madrid's *Pope Fiction*.[70] Madrid tackles common objections to the papacy, including objections that often include sensational tales rooted more in fantasy than historic facts.

## Key Text: Matthew 16:18-19

> "And I tell you, you are Peter, and on this rock I will build my Church, and the powers of death shall not prevail against it. I will give you the keys of the kingdom of heaven, and whatever you bind on earth shall be bound in heaven, and whatever you loose on earth shall be loosed in heaven."

Key Points:

1. Christ promised to build His Church upon Peter and to entrust Peter with the "keys of the kingdom."
2. Grammatically, Peter is the "rock" to which Christ referred, a point widely acknowledged even by Protestant scholars.*
3. The "keys of the kingdom" represent *royal authority*.
4. The scriptural background for Jesus' pronouncement to Peter can be found in Isaiah 22:15-23. Note that in Isaiah's prophecy, there is a dynastic office being established—that of prime minister. The king, Hezekiah, corresponds to Christ; Eliakim corresponds to Peter. The king delegates his royal authority to his prime minister as symbolized by the conferring of the keys. Note also the royal robes and the fact that the king's minister would be "*a father to the inhabitants of Jerusalem.*" Jerusalem is a foreshadowing of the Church, hence Catholics refer to the successor of St. Peter, the prime minister of the kingdom of God, as "Holy Father."

That this is indeed the backdrop to Jesus' declaration to Peter is made certain by the fact that Jesus—the very Word Incarnate—knew Scripture better than any mere mortal. He would *not* have used such imagery in a clumsy manner or with no regard for the backdrop of Old Testament symbolism.

---

* See Stephen K. Ray's *Upon This Rock* (San Francisco: Ignatius Press, 1999) for citations from the early Fathers, the Protestant Reformers and modern scholars.

Also, in the Greek text, the Greek words *petra* and *petros* differ only because it is inconceivable that Christ would confer upon Peter a feminine name (Petra). This is especially clear when we consider that the language in which Jesus originally spoke these words was *Aramaic,* in which there is only one word for "rock"—*Kepha* (from which we get the name Cephas which was also applied to Peter in Galatians 1:18 et. al.). John 1:35-42 shows that Jesus and the Apostles did, in fact, speak Aramaic, not Greek, (John's Gospel was written in Greek, but he *quotes* Jesus and His followers *speaking* Aramaic, which John in turn translates for his Greek-speaking audience).

# Other Texts:

## Luke 22:31f

*"Simon, Simon, behold, Satan demanded to have you, that he might sift you like wheat, but I have prayed for you that your faith may not fail; and when you have turned again, strengthen your brethren."*

### Key Points:
1. In the Greek text:
   a. The "you" in "sift you like wheat" is *plural*.
   b. The "you" in "I have prayed for you" is *singular*.
   c. Jesus, therefore, is saying, "Satan has demanded to sift you all (Peter and all of the disciples) but I have prayed for you (Peter) that your faith may not fail."
2. The one for whom Jesus specifically prayed is Peter (even though all the disciples were to be tested).
3. Peter would then have the responsibility to strengthen his brethren.

## John 21:15-17

*"...Jesus said to Simon Peter..."Feed my lambs...Tend my sheep...Feed my sheep..."*

### Key Points:
1. Peter is given the commission to feed the Lord's flock.
2. Jesus' words imply that Peter is to feed the entire flock (the universal Church as opposed to simply a local congregation).

# Matthew 10:2-4

*"The names of the twelve apostles are these: first, Simon, who is called Peter, and Andrew his brother; James the son of Zebedee, and John his brother...and Judas Iscariot, who betrayed him."*

### Key Points:
1. "Matthew not only lists Peter first but even calls him *first*. In Greek the word is *protos (first* or *chief).* According to William F. Ardnt and F. Wilbur Gingrich in *A Greek-English Lexicon of the New Testament and Other Early Christian Literature* '[In Matthew 10:2 this] is not meant to indicate the position of Simon in the list, since no other numbers follow, but to single him out as the *most prominent* one of the Twelve' (emphasis added). It is not insignificant, in this regard, that Judas Iscariot is listed last."[70]
2. "R.V.G. Tasker says, 'There is little doubt that *the first* (*protos*) means "first and foremost."'"[71]

The preceding passages of Scripture are just a few that demonstrate that Peter was pre-eminent among the Apostles and given a position of special authority by Christ. That Peter's position constituted an office to be occupied by successors is seen by the fact that the Church would require a visible head not only in the first generation of its existence but in every subsequent generation. Hence, it should not surprise us to find the early Fathers of the Church speaking of the Petrine primacy and pre-eminence of the bishops of Rome as the successors of St. Peter (see Appendix A).

Finally, it should be noted that the validity of the Petrine office (the papacy) guarantees infallible teaching, not impeccable conduct. Infallible teaching means the pope's teaching is protected from error. Impeccable conduct would mean that he is personally free from sin (something the Church does not teach). The pope, under certain, prescribed circumstances, is infallible. However, he is not necessarily impeccable. For example, St. Peter himself was confronted by St. Paul for hypocrisy in Galatians 2:11-13. Paul was not calling into question Peter's *teaching*. In that same epistle, Paul essentially tells us that he laid his own teaching before Peter in order to make certain that he had not been "running in vain" (Galatians 1:18-2:2). By way of an Old Covenant parallel, consider the example of Caiaphas in John 11:47-53. He was one of the leaders plotting the death of Christ, yet, as St. John tells us, he uttered prophecy by virtue of his office. The point is that the validity of an office is not lessened by the corrupt conduct of the office-holder. Therefore, as regrettable as they may be, examples of personal sins and failures on the part of popes throughout history do not in any way impugn the dignity or validity of their office.

# Appendix I

# *"Hold Fast the Traditions You Received"*

*"So then, brethren, stand firm and hold to the traditions which you were taught by us, either by word of mouth or by letter" (2 Thessalonians 2:15).*

B oth as a fundamentalist Christian and a minister in the Stone-Campbell Churches of Christ, I was taught to view the word "tradition" primarily in a negative light. The idea of religious truth being conveyed by tradition was anathematized based, ostensibly, upon our Lord's words in Matthew 15:1-9. In this exchange with the scribes and Pharisees, Jesus rebuked them for "transgress(ing) the commandment of God for the sake of (their) tradition." Moreover, He cited the prophecy of Isaiah 29:13 and applied it to them: "This people honors Me with their lips, but their heart is far from Me; in vain do they worship Me, teaching as doctrines the precepts of men."

Based upon these words of our Lord, we inferred that tradition in general was to be equated with "the precepts of men" and, therefore, viewed with suspicion if not outright contempt. There are at least two problems with this approach to tradition. On the one hand it fails to take into account the definition of the word "tradition." On the other hand, it overlooks how the word is used elsewhere in Sacred Scripture.

The English word "tradition" comes from the Latin *tradere*, which literally means, "to deliver."[73] The Greek word that is translated "tradition" in Matthew 15:2-3 is *paradosis*. It literally means "to hand over."[74] The word "tradition" does not, in and of itself, carry with it a negative connotation. It simply refers to something that has been *delivered* or *handed on*. In that sense, the Sacred Scriptures and the Christian Faith are forms of tradition because they both have been "handed on." St. Paul says as much in 2 Thessalonians 2:15 by referring to *both* his written and oral teaching as "tradition." Likewise, St. Jude refers to the entire Deposit of Faith as something that was "delivered to the saints" (Jude 3) where the word "delivered" is from the same root word as *paradosis* (tradition).

When we look at how *paradosis* (tradition) is used in the Bible, we see that it can refer to either that which is negative or that which is positive, depending upon the context. There are some traditions that are simply human in origin. These human traditions can be either good or bad depending upon their intent and effect. The "traditions of men" condemned by Christ were not condemned simply because they were of human origin. They were condemned because they were being given greater weight than the commandments of God and were being deceitfully employed as a means of circumventing the requirements of God's Law. On the other hand, there are traditions that are *apostolic* in origin and, as such, authoritative. Such is the case with the "traditions" referred to in 2 Thessalonians 2:15. Far from being condemned, they are enjoined upon the faithful with the force and weight of apostolic authority.

The preceding would seem simple enough to deduce from the Bible were it not that some translations of Scripture obscure the clear meaning of the original Greek by inconsistent translation practices. The primary case in point is the New International Version (NIV). The NIV is arguably the most popular modern English language Protestant translation of the Bible. It is widely recognized for its readability and clarity. Nonetheless, the theological bias of the translators manifests itself in a glaring manner on the topic of tradition. In virtually every instance where *paradosis* carries a negative connotation, the NIV translates it as "tradition" (cf. Matthew 15:2-6, Mark 7:3-13, Galatians 1:14, and Colossians 2:8). But whenever *paradosis* carries a positive connotation, the NIV invariably translates it as "teaching(s)" (cf. 1 Corinthians 11:2, 2 Thessalonians 2:15, and 2 Thessalonians 3:6). The net effect of such faulty translation is the propagation of an exclusively negative connotation for "tradition" despite the fact that the New Testament Scriptures themselves do otherwise.

Having seen that the Scriptures testify to the existence of tradition that is apostolic in origin (what the Catholic Church refers to as Sacred Tradition), let us now consider exactly what that Tradition is.

First of all, the Church distinguishes tradition that is apostolic in origin from that which has developed since the apostolic era. Tradition that has been handed down since apostolic times is part of the Deposit of Faith that Christ delivered to His Church, such as that referred to in Jude 3 ("the faith once and for all delivered to the saints"). It is a part of divine revelation, referred to as Sacred Tradition or simply Tradition (with an upper-case "T"). On the other hand, traditions that have developed since apostolic times are not considered to be a part of the apostolic Deposit of Faith. These would include culturally conditioned practices that, while essentially good, are not immutable or unchangeable. Placing crosses atop church steeples would be one example of this kind of "tradition."

Having said that, one question that remains is what exactly is the content of Sacred Tradition? This is an important question because anti-Catholic polemicists often scoff at the existence of Sacred Tradition and attempt to depict it as a conveniently undefined set of unwritten esoteric teachings that are produced by the Magisterium as needed. Nothing, however, could be further from the truth.

Simply put, Sacred Tradition is that which the Church has always believed and practiced. It is not, properly speaking, a form of written teaching or it would simply be a part of Sacred Scripture. Nonetheless, its existence is both witnessed to and assumed in the Sacred Scriptures.

Consider the sacrament of baptism. While we see our Lord commanding His disciples to baptize, we do not see any detailed descriptions of, or instructions pertaining to, baptism in the Scriptures. The mode of baptism is less than certain and the form of words utilized is not spelled out explicitly (See Appendix E, *The Mode of Baptism,* for a detailed study of this). Moreover, while the baptism of infants is not expressly commanded, it seems to be implied. In Colossians 2:11-12, for example, St. Paul parallels baptism to circumcision (which was, of course, administered to infants). Additionally, we see references to the baptism of entire households (e.g., Acts 16:15)—households that, presumably, had young children.

The New Testament writers assume that their readers are fully cognizant of the pertinent details. This assumption is completely reasonable because of the existence of Sacred Tradition. The Church understood what constituted valid Baptism (in terms of mode, form, and recipient) because it was already baptizing when the New Testament documents were being written.

Another way of putting it is that Sacred Tradition is the context in which the Sacred Scriptures were written and the means by which they were properly understood. Every writer of a New Testament epistle assumed the existence of a body of shared knowledge between himself and his recipients. When St. Paul wrote his first letter to the Corinthians, he began by saying, "Paul, called by the will of God to be an apostle of Christ Jesus." He did not insert a footnote and explain who Jesus Christ is. His readers already had a thorough knowledge of Jesus Christ because of the existence of Sacred Tradition (that is, the prior oral teaching that they had received). Likewise, the recipients of apostolic writings relied upon that body of shared knowledge in order to accurately understand what was written. That body of shared knowledge is what the Church commonly refers to as Sacred Tradition.

Sacred Tradition, then, can be seen as the Church's self-understanding and her understanding of the Christian faith passed on by oral teaching, her practices, and the Liturgy. The liturgy—or the worship of the Church—preserves and passes on Sacred Tradition because it is an outworking of, and thereby a witness to, the most ancient beliefs of the Church.

An illustration may serve to make the point clearer. Consider a young man, Theophilus, who, for the sake of this illustration, is an up-and-coming teacher in the Church at Corinth toward the end of the first century. While leading the congregation in a study of the first letter that St. Paul had written to them some forty years earlier, he begins to present what appears to be a novel interpretation of a particular passage. He seems to make a good case for his interpretation by appealing to sentence structure, etymology, and "common sense." As a result, a significant number of his brethren become convinced that he is on the right track. Would there be any safeguards in place to prevent the catastrophic splitting of the Church? The answer, of course, is "Yes!"

In the back of the room there is a stirring as a white-haired old man makes his way to the front. He is Theophilus' grandfather, but more importantly, he is the local bishop. He would say, "Theo, you make some interesting points. However, I was here when St. Paul wrote that letter to us, and I can tell you that you've got it all wrong."

Sacred Tradition, safeguarded by the apostolically appointed representative of the Magisterium (the bishop), made possible the preservation of the authentic meaning of Sacred Scripture. This triad of Scripture, Tradition, and the Magisterium has functioned in every generation since the founding of the Church and has served to pass on the whole and entire faith in keeping with our Lord's desire to bring Christ in His fullness to all.

# Suggested Reading

*Catechism of the Catholic Church*, Second Edition. English Translation, (copyright) 1994, United States Catholic Conference, Inc.— Libreria Editrice Vaticana.[*]

Adams, Karl, *Roots of the Reformation,* Zanesville, OH: CHResources, 2000.

Butler, Scott, Norman Dahlgren and David Hess, *Jesus, Peter & the Keys: A Scriptural Handbook on the Papacy.* Santa Barbara, Calif.: Queenship Publishing, 1996.

Dale, James W., *Judaic Baptism: An Inquiry into the Meaning of the Word as Determined by the Usage of Jewish and Patristic Writers.* Phillipsburg, N.J.: P & R Publishing, 1991.

Father Mateo, *Refuting the Attack on Mary.* San Diego, CA: Catholic Answers, 1999.

Graham, Henry G., *Where We Got the Bible.* San Diego: Catholic Answers, 1997.

Grodi, Marcus, *How Firm a Foundation,* Zanesville, OH: CHResources, 2002.

[*] The *Catechism of the Catholic Church* is the official and authoritative presentation of the Catholic faith promulgated by the Vatican. Even non-Catholics often find its commentary and instruction to be both informative and enlightening. It is readily available at major bookstores and from organizations like the *Coming Home Network International* and *Catholic Answers*.

Grodi, Marcus, *Journeys Home, Revised and Updated,* Zanesville, OH: CHResources, 2005.

Howard, Thomas, *Evangelical Is Not Enough.* San Francisco: Ingatius Press, 1988.

Jurgens, William A., *The Faith of the Early Fathers.* Collegeville, Minn.: The Liturgical Press, 1979. An excellent compilation of writings of the early Christian writings.

Keating, Karl, *Catholicism and Fundamentalism: The Attack on "Romanism" by "Bible Christians."* San Francisco: Ignatius Press, 1988.

Keating, Karl, *What Catholics* Really *Believe – Setting the Record Straight.* Ann Arbor, Mich.: Servant Publications, 1992.

Oatis, Gregory, *Catholic Doctrine in Scripture,* Zanesville, OH: CHResources, 2003.

Ray, Stephen K., *Upon This Rock.* San Francisco: Ignatius Press, 1999.

Shea, Mark P., *By What Authority?* Huntington, Ind.: Our Sunday Visitor Publishing Division, 1996.

Shea, Mark P., *This is My Body.* (Front Royal, Va.: Christendom Press, 1993.

## Recommended Resources

For apologetics and questions about the Catholic Faith:

**Catholic Answers**
2020 Gillespie Way
El Cajon, CA  92020
(619) 387-7200
www.catholic.com

For information and support for Protestants, clergy and laity, considering the Catholic faith:

**The Coming Home Network International**
P.O. Box 8290
Zanesville, OH  43702
(740) 450-1175
www.chnetwork.org

For Catholic apologetical and catechetical teaching tapes and videos:

**St. Joseph Communications**
P.O. Box 1911, Ste 83
Tehachapi, CA  93581
(800) 526-2151
www.saintjoe.com

For Catholic spiritual formation materials by Father John A. Hardon, S.J.:

> **Eternal Life**
> P.O. Box 787
> Bardstown, KY 40004
> (800) 842-2871
> www.lifeeternal.org

For Catholic television programming:

> **Eternal Word Television Network**
> 5817 Old Leeds Road
> Irondale, AL 35210-2198
> (270) 271-2900
> www.ewtn.org (Live and archived programming available on the web)

For information on Natural Family Planning and the Catholic teaching on marital chastity:

> **The Couple to Couple League International**
> P.O. Box 111184
> Cincinnati, OH 45211-1184
> (513) 471-2000
> www.ccli.org

# Endnotes

[1] Information obtained from the Old Mulkey Meeting House website of the Kentucky Department of State Parks (http://parks.ky.gov/mulkey.htm).

[2] "The Old Mulkey Meeting House," Clayton E. Gooden, *Discipliana*, January 1965, *Discipliana* is the official journal of the Disciples of Christ Historical Society.

[3] Keating, Karl. *Catholicism and Fundamentalism: The Attack on "Romanism" by "Bible Christians"*, San Francisco: Ignatius Press, 1988.

[4] *Ibid*, p. 296.

[5] Readers can learn more about the Fathers of Mercy by visiting their Website (www.fathersofmercy.com). Inquiries concerning vocations and parish missions can also be made at the Website or by writing them at Fathers of Mercy, 806 Shaker Museum Rd., Auburn, KY 42206.

[6] The Disciples of Christ Historical Society in Nashville, Tennessee, gathers, preserves, and makes accessible the historical documents of the Stone-Campbell movement. Readers can visit the society's Website at www.dishistsoc.org.

[7] *This Rock* magazine is a monthly magazine of apologetics and evangelization published by Catholic Answers in El Cajon, CA. Their Website is www.catholic.com.

[8] *The Coming Home Network International* can be contacted at P.O. Box 8290, Zanesville, OH 43702, on the Web at www.chnetwork.org. or by calling (740) 450-1175. The founder of the *CHNetwork*, Marcus Grodi, is a former Presbyterian minister and the host of the weekly television program, *The Journey Home*, and radio program, *Deep In Scripture*, both broadcast internationally on the Eternal Word Television Network (EWTN).

⁹ Tolle, James M. *The Church, Apostasy, Reformation, and Restoration,* Pasadena, Texas; Haun Publishing Co., p. 3.

¹⁰ *Ibid,* p. 6.

¹¹ MGeisler, Norman L. and Nix, William E. *A General Introduction to the Bible*; Moody Press, Chicago, Illinois. pp. 291-293.

¹² Glossary of the *Catechism of the Catholic Church (*p. 898*).*

¹³ *Catechism of the Catholic Church, no. 1127.*

¹⁴ *Ibid, no. 1324.*

¹⁵ Pohle, J. "The Real Presence of Christ in the Eucharist," *Catholic Encyclopedia*, Vol. V, Robert Appleton Co., available on-line at www.newadvent.org, 1909.

¹⁶ *Ibid.*

¹⁷ Justin Martyr. *First Apology*, 66 (A.D. 151).

¹⁸ St. Ignatius of Antioch. *Letter to the Ephesians* (A.D. 110).

¹⁹ St. Ignatius of Antioch. *Letter to the Smyrnaeans* (A.D. 110).

²⁰ St. Justin Martyr. *First Apology* (A.D. 150).

²¹ *Letter to the Smyrneans,* (A.D. 110).

²² Jurgens, W.A. *The Faith of the Early Fathers*, Vol. 1, Collegeville, Minn: The Liturgical Press, 1970, p. 167

²³ Tertullian. AD UXOREM, II, VIII, 6-8: CCL, I, 393 (As cited by Pope John Paul II in *Familiaris Consortio).*

²⁴ *Catechism of the Catholic Church*, Glossary, p. 903.

²⁵ *Ibid,* p. 903.

²⁶ The answer of the Baltimore Catechism to the question, "Why did God make me?", 1941.

²⁷ St. John Chrysostom. *"Virginity"*, X: PG 48: 540 (Cited in CCC, No. 1620).

²⁸ *CCC*, No. 1638.

²⁹ cf. *CCC*, No. 1601, 1638–1641.

³⁰ *CCC*, No. 1954.

³¹ *CCC,* paragraph 2362.

³² *Webster's New Universal Unabridged Dictionary*, Cleveland: Simon & Schuster, 1983.

³³ *CCC*, No. 2366–2370.

³⁴ *CCC*, No. 1030 and 1031.

³⁵ *CCC*, No. 1021.

[36] *CCC*, No. 1035.

[37] *CCC*, No. 1855.

[38] Hardon, John A. *Modern Catholic Dictionary*, Bardstown, KY: Eternal Life, 1999, p. 559.

[39] Hardon, John A. *Modern Catholic Dictionary*, p. 202.

[40] Boettner, Loraine. *Roman Catholicism*, Philadelphia, PA: The Presbyterian and Reformed Publishing Co., 1962, pp 7-9.

[41] The Catechism is citing from Tertullian, *De Paenit*. 4, 2: PL 1, 1343.

[42] Roberts, Alexander and Donaldson, James. *Nicene and Post-Nicene Fathers, Second Series: Volume X*, Oak Harbor, WA: Logos Research Systems, Inc., 1997.

[43] *Ibid, Volume II.*

[44] *Ibid.*

[45] Christian Classics Ethereal Library (www.ccel.org).

[46] Roberts, Alexander and Donaldson, James. *Ante-Nicene Fathers: Volume V*, Oak Harbor, WA: Logos Research Systems, Inc. 1997.

[47] *Ibid, Volume VIII.*

[48] Geisler and Nix. *A General Introduction to the Bible*, Chicago: Moody Press, 1986, p. 269.

[49] The reader can view a digital copy of this famous Bible online at www.gutenbergdigital.de/gudi/start.htm.

[50] Conant, T.J. *The Meaning and Use of BAPTIZE IN Philologically and Historically Investigated*, for the American Bible Union, New York: American Bible Union, 1877.

[51] *Ibid*, p 2

[52] *Ibid*, p 7.

[53] *Ibid*, pp 7-8.

[54] Dale, John W. *Classic Baptism*, Phillipsburg, N.J., Presbyterian and Reformed Publishers, 1989, p. 287.

[55] *Ibid*, p. 228

[56] *Ibid*, p. 291.

[57] *Ibid*, p. 299.

[58] *Ibid*, p. 304.

[59] *Ibid*, p. 306.

[60] *Ibid,* p. 354.

[61] For more on this see James W. Dale, *Judaic Baptism*, Wm. Rutter, pp. 169–217.

[62] *Textus Receptus* and *Byzantine Majority Text.*

[63] Ward, Rowland S. *Baptism in Scripture and History: A Fresh Study of the Meaning and Mode of Baptism,* Victoria, Australia: Rowland S. Ward, 1991, p. 43.

[64] *Ibid,* p. 44.

[65] *The Sixteen Documents of Vatican II,* Boston: Pauline Books and Media, 1999, p. 418.

[66] *Ibid.*

[67] Butler, Scott, Dahlgren, Norman, and Hess, David. *Jesus, Peter & the Keys: A Scriptural Handbook on the Papacy*, Santa Barbara, Calif.: Queenship Publishing Co., 1996.

[68] Ray, Stephen K. *Upon This Rock*, San Francisco: Ignatius Press, 1999.

[69] Madrid, Patrick. *Pope Fiction*, 1999 Basilica Press, 1999.

[70] Ray, *Upon This Rock*, p. 30 (footnote 26).

[71] *Ibid.*

[72] *Webster's New Twentieth Century Dictionary*, Second Edition, New York: Simon & Schuster, 1983.

[73] W.E. Vine, *An Expository Dictionary of Biblical Words*, Nashville: Thomas Nelson Publishers, 1985.